Wise Therapy

Other titles in the School of Psychotherapy and Counselling (SPC) Series of Regent's College:

Heart of Listening   Rosalind Pearmain
Embodied Theories   Ernesto Spinelli and Sue Marshall (eds)

SPC SERIES

Wise Therapy
Philosophy for Counsellors

Tim LeBon

CONTINUUM
London and New York

Continuum

The Tower Building
11 York Road
London SE1 7NX

370 Lexington Avenue
New York
NY 10017-6503

www.continuumbooks.com

First published 2001

British Library Cataloguing-in-Publication Data
A catalogue record for this book is available from the British Library.

ISBN 0–8264–5782–7 (hardback)
ISBN 0–8264–5207–8 (paperback)

Designed and typeset by Kenneth Burnley, Wirral, Cheshire
Printed and bound in Great Britain by Biddles Ltd, *www.biddles.co.uk*

Contents

Series Editor's Introduction

I T IS BOTH A GREAT HONOUR AND A PLEASURE to welcome readers to the SPC Series.

The School of Psychotherapy and Counselling at Regent's College (SPC) is one of the largest and most widely respected psychotherapy, counselling and counselling psychology training institutes in the UK. The SPC Series published by Continuum marks a major development in the School's mission to initiate and develop novel perspectives centred upon the major topics of debate within the therapeutic professions so that their impact and influence upon the wider social community may be more adequately understood and assessed.

A brief overview of SPC

Although its origins lie in an innovative study programme developed by Antioch University, USA, in 1977, SPC has been in existence in its current form since 1990. SPC's MA in Psychotherapy and Counselling programme obtained British validation with City University in 1991. More recently, the MA in Existential Counselling Psychology obtained accreditation from the British Psychological Society. SPC was also the first UK institute to develop a research-based MPhil/PhD programme in Psychotherapy and Counselling, and this has been validated by City University since 1992. Largely on the impetus of its first Dean, Emmy van Deurzen, SPC became a full training and accrediting member of the United Kingdom Council for Psychotherapy (UKCP) and continues to maintain a strong and active presence in that organization through its Professional Members, many of whom also hold professional affiliations with the British Psychological Society (BPS), the British Association of Counselling and Psychotherapy (BACP), the Society for Existential Analysis (SEA) and the European Society for Communicative Psychotherapy (ESCP).

SPC's other programmes include: a Foundation Certificate in Psychotherapy and Counselling, Advanced Professional Diploma Programmes in Existential Psychotherapy and Integrative Psychotherapy, and a series of intensive Continuing Professional Development and related Adjunct courses such as its innovative Legal and Family Mediation Programmes.

With the personal support of the President of Regent's College, Mrs Gillian Payne, SPC has recently established the Psychotherapy and Counselling Consultation Centre housed on the college campus which provides individual and group therapy for both private individuals and organizations.

As a unique centre for learning and professional training, SPC has consistently emphasized the comparative study of psychotherapeutic theories and techniques while paying careful and accurate attention to the philosophical assumptions underlying the theories being considered and the philosophical coherence of those theories to their practice-based standards and professional applications within a diversity of private and public settings. In particular, SPC fosters the development of faculty and graduates who think independently, are theoretically well informed and able skilfully and ethically to apply the methods of psychotherapy and counselling in practice, in the belief that knowledge advances through criticism and debate, rather than by uncritical adherence to received wisdom.

The integrative attitude of SPC

The underlying ethos upon which the whole of SPC's educational and training programme rests is its *integrative attitude*, which can be summarized as follows:

There exists a multitude of perspectives in current psychotherapeutic thought and practice, each of which expresses a particular philosophical viewpoint on an aspect of being human. No one single perspective or set of underlying values and assumptions is universally shared.

Given that a singular, or shared, view does not exist, SPC seeks to enable a learning environment which allows competing and diverse models to be considered both conceptually and experientially so that their areas of interface and divergence can be exposed, considered and clarified. This aim espouses the value of holding the tension between contrasting and often contradictory ideas, of 'playing with' their experiential possibilities and of allowing a paradoxical security which can 'live with' and at times even thrive in the absence of final and fixed truths.

SPC defines this aim as 'the integrative attitude' and has designed all of its courses so that its presence will challenge and stimulate all aspects of our students' and trainees' learning experience. SPC believes that this deliberate engagement with difference should be reflected in the manner in which the faculty relate to students, clients and colleagues at all levels. In such a way this attitude may be seen as the lived expression of the foundational ethos of SPC.

The SPC Series

The series evolved out of a number of highly encouraging and productive discussions between Publishing Director at Continuum Books, Mr Robin Baird-Smith, and the present Academic Dean of SPC, Professor Ernesto Spinelli.

From the start, it was recognized that SPC, through its faculty and Professional Members, was in a unique position to provide a series of wide-ranging, accessible and pertinent texts intended to challenge, inspire and influence debate in a variety of issues and areas central to therapeutic enquiry. Further, SPC's focus and concern surrounding the ever more pervasive impact of therapeutic ideas and practices upon all sections of contemporary society highlighted the worth, if not necessity, of a series that could address key topics from an informed, critical and non-doctrinal perspective.

The publication of the first three texts in the series during 2001 marks the beginning of what is hoped will be a long and fruitful relationship between SPC and Continuum. More than that, there exists the hope that the series will become identified by professionals and public alike as an invaluable contributor to the advancement of psychotherapy and counselling as a vigorously self-critical, socially minded, and humane profession.

PROFESSOR ERNESTO SPINELLI
Series Editor

Preface

F OR THE GREEKS, philosophy was a way of life, almost a religion, and after a hiatus of nearly 2,000 years it may be that philosophy is on the brink of once again making a significant contribution to human well-being. It might just turn out that a major contribution will come through the fruitful marriage of philosophy and counselling. The great ancient Greek philosopher Socrates engaged in philosophical dialogue in a way reminiscent of a challenging modern philosophical counsellor. Later, Stoics and Epicureans developed philosophical 'spiritual' exercises reminiscent of the homework exercises modern-day cognitive therapists hand out to clients. Some of this ancient wisdom has already been mined by counsellors: plenty remains waiting to be shown the light of day. Philosophy has come a long way since the Greeks' contribution, particularly in the last 50 years. Academic philosophers have advanced our understanding of many important topics such as the nature of right and wrong and well-being, and have developed fine-tuned philosophical techniques of analysis. Applied philosophers have increasingly been using these insights and techniques to help sort out ethical issues in the public domain, such as animal rights and euthanasia. A growing number of philosophers – philosophical practitioners – have taken this a stage further, and begun helping individuals use philosophy in counselling, management and educational settings.

Modern philosophers have even more to offer than the great Greek philosophers. But do *counsellors* need philosophy? My view, confirmed by training and practice in existential, cognitive, philosophical and integrative forms of counselling, is that although Rogerian empathy helps people considerably, aided and abetted by philosophical insights and techniques it can help them even more. Equally, philosophers working in counselling can benefit considerably from the ideas and experience of those philosophically minded therapists – cognitive and existential counsellors and logotherapists – who have been applying philosophy to counselling for some time now. The time is ripe for a synthesis of the acceptable ideas of philosophers working in counselling, and counsellors working with philosophy. One of the aims of this book is to develop such a synthesis.

On a more personal note, this book is a result of my desire to share and further explore what I believe are the exciting possibilities of both philosophy and counselling. Since my first ventures into philosophy as an Oxford undergraduate over twenty years ago, I have always felt that it is its *practical* potential that makes philosophy really important. My experience as a counsellor has confirmed both the need for helping people with 'problems in living' and the potential for the counselling room to be an arena where people can be helped. My experience suggested something else as well. The different approaches to counselling all seemed to help, but in different ways. What if a therapy could be developed which took the strengths of each, developing them into a coherent whole, applying only appropriate ideas and methods at the right time? The idea of integrative therapy is not a new one, but the idea of basing such an integrative therapy on acceptable philosophical theories and techniques may be. This is the project I set myself to develop in my counselling work. This book is a statement of where that project stands at the moment.

There is a large number of people without whom this project would not have been possible. I am indebted to many at Regent's College. Most of all I must thank Ernesto Spinelli for his encouragement and ideas as Series Editor. I must also mention Simon du Plock, who first suggested the idea of the book and helped me create the BA module which set the ball rolling for this book. I would also like to thank all my tutors, students and clients, and my colleagues in the Society of Existential Analysis, for their stimulating contributions over the years. More recently my colleagues in the Society of Consultant Philosophy and those who contribute to its journal, *Practical Philosophy*, which I edit, have formed a constant source of stimulating discussion. Last, but certainly not least, particular thanks are due to the man whose inspiring tutorials made me realize the value of philosophy, Mike Inwood, my tutor at Trinity College, Oxford.

I would also like to thank those at Continuum for their efficient and professional work, especially David Hayden for his fine editorial work and Robin Baird-Smith for his faith in the project in its early days. I would particularly like to thank my colleagues David Arnaud and Antonia Macaro for their enlightening discussions on various areas of counselling and practical philosophy. The Progress model, which features in this book, is very much a joint development, and I am grateful for their permission to use it in this book. I would also like to thank those who have read all or part of the book for their insightful comments, including Bill Anderson, David Arnaud, Shamil Chandaria, Robert Hill, Antonia Macaro and Freddie Strasser. The book is better for their comments, which is not to say that they agree with all of it! Some of the material used in this book has appeared before. I would like to thank *The Philosophers' Magazine*, *Philosophy Now* and *Humanity* for their permission to reprint these items. Finally, I would like to thank my family for their support and encouragement throughout this project, especially my wife Beata, to whom this book is dedicated.

TIM LEBON
Guildford, Surrey
January 2001

To Beata

1 | Wise Therapy: An Introductory Overview

Wise therapy

Brian is sad and sometimes gets depressed, but most of all wonders how he has come to lose touch with all that he used to think important. Claire is a young psychology undergraduate with a career decision looming over her. Torn between pursuing a traditional career and trying to do something more meaningful with her life, such as becoming a counsellor, she is suffering much anguish and anxiety over the decision. Alex, a dying woman with six months to live, urgently wants the opportunity to take stock of her life.

In previous eras, Brian, Claire and Alex may well have gone to their priest or family for help. In the twenty-first century they are just as likely to seek help through counselling. These people do not need to have their unconscious interpreted, or be clinically diagnosed.[1] A listening ear may help, but is it alone sufficient to help them make good decisions, understand the language of their emotions and work out how to lead a meaningful and worthwhile life? More than anything, Brian, Claire and Alex are in need of wise therapy: but have counsellors got the tools and knowledge to be wise therapists?[2]

Linda has been approached by a couple wanting to take advantage of the low-cost therapy she offers, but she is unsure whether it is ethical to branch out into couple counselling, for which she has no specific training. The latest revelation of Ian's client's inner world leaves him with a dilemma about whether confidentiality extends to clients who are potential child-molesters. Both of these practitioners realize that to be wise therapists, they need an area of expertise not covered by training programmes focusing on communication skills and psychological theories alone.

Susan is a counsellor trying to defend counselling against the attacks of her smug anti-therapy psychiatrist friend, Graham. 'Empirical studies show that counselling is not a cost-effective way of helping people, and it would be quite wrong to provide public money to subsidize it' says Graham triumphantly. Susan is sure that there must be a good answer – but is lost for words. How she would like to be a wise therapist who could put such doubters in their place.

What is philosophy and why is it relevant to counselling?

We would all like to be wise therapists. The question is, how can we achieve this? In this book I intend to show how *philosophy* can help. Philosophy can help counsellors in three ways – in informing work with clients like Brian, Claire and Alex, in helping with therapists' own dilemmas, like those faced by Linda and Ian, and in assessing the theoretical foundations and benefits of counselling. To back up this assertion we need to go a little more deeply into the nature of philosophy. The *Oxford Companion to Philosophy* defines philosophy as

> rationally critical thinking, of a more or less systematic kind
> about the general nature of the world (metaphysics or theory
> of existence), the justification of belief (epistemology or theory of
> knowledge) and the conduct of life (ethics or theory of value).
> (Honderich, 1995)

This definition brings out three important elements of philosophy – its subject matter, its methods and its systematic nature – all of which are relevant to counselling.

The subject matter of philosophy

The *Oxford Companion* correctly identifies three major philosophical topics – the general nature of the world, the justification of belief and the conduct of life. All of these are germane to counselling and will be discussed in this book. The question of the meaning of life is perhaps the most fundamental of all metaphysical questions. Logotherapists, inspired by Viktor Frankl, have long argued that the most effective form of therapy is through enhancing meaning. We will look at the question of the meaning of life and go on to explore how therapy can enhance meaning. The justification of belief can sometimes be the matter of esoteric debate in the branch of philosophy called epistemology. However, we will be focusing very much on the practical questions of how clients' beliefs, preferences and decisions can become more rational and therefore allow the client to live in a more satisfying way. We will also explore the extent to which beliefs and evaluations are relevant to the emotions and the ways in which philosophy can help counsellors construct a better theory of the emotions and help clients move toward emotional wisdom. The conduct of life, the final area of philosophy mentioned by the *Oxford Companion*, encompasses questions about well-being and right and wrong. Theories about well-being allow us to evaluate the value of counselling and help us clarify and, where appropriate, challenge the values held by clients. Finally, philosophical ideas about right and wrong assist counsellors faced with ethical dilemmas and help them facilitate clients' decision-making when faced with either prudential or ethical dilemmas.

Philosophical methods

The *Oxford Companion*'s reference to 'rationally critical thinking' accurately implies that philosophers use reasoning and argument rather than mere assertion, observation or experiment to enable them to attempt to answer the questions of philosophy identified above. We need to go beyond this brief definition and identify specific philosophical methods in order to demystify philosophy and make it more accessible to the non-specialist. The five philosophical methods that I have found most useful in both the theory and practice of counselling are:

1. critical thinking;
2. conceptual analysis;
3. phenomenology;
4. thought experiments;
5. creative thinking.

We will be returning to these methods throughout the text; here I will set the scene by saying a little about each method and its use in counselling and this book.

1. Critical thinking[3]
Critical thinking involves testing whether arguments stand up to critical investigation and seeing whether we have good reason to accept them. We will use critical thinking to assess philosophical theories and also investigate the extent to which critical thinking can help clients toward emotional wisdom, good decisions and enlightened values. Critical thinking's practical value is now widely recognized and it is increasingly being taught as part of school curricula. Adult counsellors who may have missed out on this education owe it to their clients to be familiar with critical thinking skills, at the very least so they can assess whether to incorporate them into their work. Chapter 6 contains a method for using critical thinking that has been specially adapted for use in counselling.

2. Conceptual analysis
Conceptual analysis is a way of becoming clearer about what we mean. It involves a careful investigation of language and usage and includes searching for definitions and drawing distinctions. The conceptual analysis of evaluative terms such as 'autonomy'

is important when discussing the benefits of counselling, as we shall see in Chapter 2. Similarly, in Chapter 5 we shall see how conceptual analysis of the meaning of life can help prevent confusions which can be a matter of life and death for clients. As well as benefiting from the conceptual analysis carried out by past philosophers, philosophically informed counsellors can use conceptual analysis in sessions to help clarify client issues. Chapter 6 also provides a method to help you carry out conceptual analysis.

3. Phenomenology

Because of its use in existential–phenomenological and Rogerian counselling, phenomenology is perhaps the philosophical method most familiar to counsellors, but also the one most likely to be the subject of controversy and debate. I will be using the term in the way normally understood by counsellors. This sees phenomenology as 'a philosophy arguing that events and objects are to be understood in terms of our immediate experience of them as they appear to us' (Feltham and Dryden, 1993). Spinelli (1989) has described the phenomenological method used in counselling in three steps – epoché, description and horizontalization. These three complementary steps mean first trying to set aside our assumptions and biases, then limiting oneself to describing rather than explaining, and finally treating each item as being of equal potential value. The goal of phenomenology is perhaps most simply understood as a concern for the client's own subjective meanings. This usually means staying with the client's material – 'being with the client'. It also can mean prompting the client for more information to gain a more complete understanding of their subjective meanings. To investigate personal meaning thoroughly, one needs to ask questions, but these tend to be 'What?' 'When?' and 'How?' questions rather than 'Why?'[4] (phenomenologists are *not* trying to explain things). Phenomenology is vital in ensuring that the client feels understood (thus strengthening the therapeutic alliance) and in helping the client and counsellor to work

together on the client's issues. If the counsellor does not understand the client's subjective meanings and experience, he or she
is unlikely to be very helpful.

4. Thought experiments

A thought experiment is an experiment carried out, not in the
laboratory, but in our minds. Probably the most well-known
thought experiment in the history of philosophy is Descartes'
imagining that an evil genius might be deceiving him about all
his thoughts and experiences, an experiment Descartes used to
attempt to establish the secure foundations of knowledge. In
counselling, as well as helping to find exceptions to clients'
'stuck' thinking, thought experiments can be a vivid and interesting way of exploring what really matters to clients. For
example, the Dutch philosophical counsellor Ad Hoogendijk
(Hoogendijk, 1995) suggests that career-counselling clients
map out a 'Life Design', in which they consider their life in five-
or ten-year periods between the present time and when they are
80. For each period they should consider where and how they
want to live, what relationships they want and what activities they
want to be doing, paying no attention to practical limitations. As
Hoogendijk says, 'through the life-design, the career counsellor,
together with the counselee, can help translate the latter's most
valued qualities of life into attainable goals and strategies'.[5]

5. Creative thinking

Creative thinking methods such as brainstorming and lateral
thinking have long been part of the management trainee's cur-
riculum (e.g. de Bono, 1982) but have only recently begun to
percolate through to philosophy via the practical ethics literature. Creative thinking turns out to be the perfect complement
to critical thinking. Whilst critical thinking helps one assess
arguments, creative thinking is needed to think them up in the
first place. As we shall see, creative thinking helps us both to find
'the best problem' (Weston, 1997) and 'win–win' solutions to
problems (Covey, 1992). Creative thinking methods have con-

siderable potential for helping with client problem-solving and dealing with rigid and sedimented patterns of thought.

These five methods are the nuts and bolts of the philosopher's toolbox. We will be using these methods throughout this book to assess philosophical theories and exploring ways in which they can inform a counsellor's work. They also form the building-blocks for other philosophical methods. We will be looking at my RSVP method that is used in values counselling and the Progress procedure developed by David Arnaud, Antonia Macaro and myself to help in decision counselling. These will be described fully in Chapter 6.

Philosophy's systematic nature and its attempt to provide answers

The final feature of philosophy to which the *Oxford Companion*'s definition draws our attention is its systematic nature. Philosophers have always used philosophical methods to try to build systems that contain a coherent, consistent and correct answer to the questions of philosophy. We will indeed be looking at some of the answers that famous philosophers have given about the nature of well-being, right and wrong, the emotions and the meaning of life. One inspiring view of philosophy is to see it as providing the 'wisdom of the ages', gathering dust in deserted libraries, urgently awaiting our attention to extract its lessons to enhance modern life. This is broadly the approach taken by Alain de Botton in his highly recommended *The Consolations of Philosophy* (de Botton, 2000). The only problem is that, particularly when it comes to the fundamental questions we are dealing with in the present book, no one has yet come up with a theory that has met with anything like universal acceptance. For example, although utilitarianism is a very well-known answer to questions about what is right or wrong, stating that right actions are those that produce the largest quantity of total happiness, first-year philosophy undergraduates soon learn of a whole host of formidable criticisms.[6] This can be very off-putting to would-be philosophers, who soon conclude that philosophy cannot deliver its promises.

How then are we counsellors to treat philosophical systems? The approach taken in this book is to examine each theory critically. If a theory is found to be acceptable, then we can use it – if not, we take the view that most theories contain at least part of the truth and try to construct an acceptable theory out of the admissible elements of each. The emergent theories of well-being, the emotions, right and wrong and the meaning of life can then be used to help the client toward emotional wisdom, good decisions and enlightened values and assess philosophical assumptions made by theories of counselling. For example, the theoretical discussion of well-being and values informs RSVP, an integrated procedure for helping clients explore and develop their values. There is, of course, a danger in all this – namely that the theories that we end up accepting might themselves be flawed. This is an occupational hazard of philosophy, the results of which are unlikely to achieve scientific status. I believe that the best way to use philosophical systems in counselling is to accept that they are a body of ideas rather than a body of knowledge. Philosophical ideas should be put forward tentatively as part of a genuine dialogue with clients, rather than prescribed as an authoritative solution. As counsellors faced with the necessary task of helping the many clients in distress, we must navigate the rocky path between van Deurzen-Smith's (1994) worthy plea for counsellors to 'seriously investigat[e] what life is about and what people can do to live it better' and Wittgenstein's cautionary dictum that 'What we cannot speak about we must pass over in silence' (1921).

A philosophical attitude

One notable aspect of philosophy not brought out by the *Oxford Companion*'s definition is philosophy's enquiring attitude or spirit. Socrates' suggestion that 'the unexamined life is not worth living' sums up this enquiring attitude. Those who still have the sense of wonder they had as children, and those not easily satisfied by superficial answers, exemplify this philosophical spirit. In counselling, this enquiring attitude can provide vital motivation for client and counsellor alike. Just as patients in long-term psychoanalysis are motivated by curiosity about their unconscious, clients in philosophical counselling are spurred on by a quest to gain a philosophical understanding of their life.

Philosophical counselling and other philosophical forms of counselling

A central aim of this book, though, is to show how philosophy can contribute to counselling *practice*. A number of enlightened counsellors have of course been applying philosophical methods and ideas for some time. Philosophical counsellors, existential–phenomenological counsellors, cognitive therapists and logotherapists come into this category. These four approaches will all be discussed at greater length in the text; here I will introduce each type of counselling and say a little about the ways in which they are philosophical.[7]

Philosophical counselling (PC)

One of the most significant recent developments in this area has been the growth of philosophical counselling (PC), a type of counselling that uses philosophical insights and methods to help people think through significant issues in their life. These issues tend to be non-pathological 'problems in living' such as questions around direction in life, relationship issues, ethical problems and career dilemmas. The Israeli philosophical counsellor Ran Lahav (1995) has influentially suggested that all philosophical counselling involves 'worldview interpretation'. By a 'worldview' is meant someone's philosophy of life; worldview interpretation refers to the process of uncovering worldviews, reflecting on them, and applying them to the problem at hand. PC's roots go back at least as far as Socrates, whose dialogues with his fellow Athenians about ethical issues such as justice, friendship and piety have famously been recorded by Plato.[8] For the ancients, the idea that philosophy could be anything but practical would have seemed very strange. As Epicurus said, 'Empty is the argument of the philosopher which does not relieve any human suffering.' However, since Descartes philosophy has focused far more on the foundations of theoretical knowledge than the practical application of philosophy to everyday life. Only recently has there been renewed interest in applied philosophy (e.g. Singer, 1979). This, combined with the social acceptance of counselling as a non-medical way of helping people deal with non-pathological problems, created the milieu in which modern PC could be established. The German philosopher Gerd Achenbach is usually credited as the first modern philosophical counsellor, and the date of 1981 given as PC's birth – this is when Achenbach first opened his philosophical practice in Cologne, Germany to what he called 'visitors'. Philosophical counselling has since spread over the world, for example to Holland, Israel, Canada, the United Kingdom and perhaps most notably to the United States where much publicity has surrounded Lou Marinoff and his book *Plato Not Prozac!* In Britain the rise of philosophical counselling owes much to the Society of Consultant Philosophers (SCP), which organized the Fifth International Conference on Philosophy in Practice in Oxford in 1999 and keeps a register of qualified philosophical counsellors.[9]

The way that philosophical counselling works is best illustrated by means of a case vignette. Alex, a dying atheist, describes her reason for seeking PC as follows:

> Time is very precious for me, as I have been told that I have only six months to live. I'm an atheist, so don't want to go to a priest to help me face up to death. However I do feel the urgent need to take stock of my life and really try to make the most of what is left. Would philosophical counselling be worth my time?[10]

The exact course of philosophical counselling would depend very much on what Alex wanted. For some clients, having a space to reflect for themselves is the most important aspect, whereas others specifically want to have their perspective challenged philosophically. Alex's initial statement implies that, like most people, she wants a mixture of support and challenge; with matters of life and death, particular sensitivity is obviously called for. What follows is a sketch of one route that philosophical counselling with Alex might take.

Alex talks of facing up to death, so a good place to start would be an enquiry into the nature of death. Being an atheist, Alex would probably dismiss the notion of an after-life out of hand, but it would be worth checking the grounds for this dismissal. Does she want to make the strong claim that the idea of living after one's body has ceased to function is incoherent, or the more modest assertion that we have no good reason to believe in an after-life? Shakespeare (through Hamlet) suggested that death is 'the undiscovered country from whose bourn no traveller returns', but philosophical reflection might cast doubt on speaking about death as a country, even metaphorically. Epicurus, for one, maintained that 'When death is there, we are not, and when we are there, death is not.' The question that Alex would be asked to consider is whether death is a state of oneself (like being unconscious) or a non-state (like before we were conceived). The distinction is important, because, as Hamlet recognized, the thought of being in a completely different state is indeed frightening. Epicurus argued that since death isn't something we experience, there is no good reason to be anxious about it. Epicurus' argument is reinforced by Lucretius' comparison of the time after we die with the time before we were born; we don't consider the aeons before we were born a disaster, so why should we think differently about the period following our death? (Alex might be referred to Nagel's excellent *Mortal Questions* (1979) or *What Does It All Mean?* (1987) if she wanted to pursue these questions further.)

Such discussion could well convince Alex that an atheist has a lot less to fear from death than a Christian, who may indeed have grounds for anguishing about the possibility of hell-fire. But she might complain that we haven't yet addressed her main concern, which is more to do with the absence of the positive benefits of living than the negative aspects of death itself. Some philosophers (notably Bernard Williams) have argued that immortality would not really be such a good thing; it would be very boring. It's hard to imagine being persuaded by this argument, but perhaps a Kantian thought experiment asking 'What would it be like if everyone lived for ever?' might give pause for thought. Clearly, if we did all go on living, there would be insufficient resources for future generations; what's more, if previous generations had been bestowed the gift of immortality, it's highly unlikely that any of us would have lived at all. Perhaps dying is our ultimate, albeit involuntary, gift to future generations.

Richard Dawkins has argued that in a sense we *are* immortal; through the transmission of our genes and memes. If Alex has children, her genes will survive; in any case her memes – replicants of her ideas – will continue their existence. If she has written a poem, contributed to a movement, or just passed on her ideas to her friends and family then to the extent that she *is* these thoughts she will carry on living. Alex might well counter this by saying that it blurs the distinction between her memes and her*self*. She might well sympathize with Woody Allen, who said 'I don't want to achieve immortality through my work . . . I want to achieve it through not dying.'

If this was her reaction, we could usefully move from talking about death to talking about life. Alex said she wants to make the most of the time she has left, so how can she do this? A philosophical counsellor is particularly well equipped to help someone think through what really matters to them. A starting point for Alex might be a consideration of what atheistic philosophers have thought. Did she agree with Richard Robinson's (1964) list of values in his classic work *An Atheist's Values* – beauty, truth, reason and love? What in *her* life had she found to be of most value? Such a dialogue would serve two purposes – to allow Alex to take stock of her life, and also to think about how to use her remaining time as best she could. We might even discuss the concept of a 'good death' – what would she have to do between now and the time she died to feel that she had done as much as she could?

Existential therapist Irvin Yalom has noticed in his work with terminally ill cancer patients that there is often a rearrangement of life's priorities, an enhanced sense of living in the present, a deeper communication with loved ones and more willingness to take risks. Alex's interest in philosophical counselling might well reflect the fact that this 'trivializing of the trivial' has already begun. Philosophical counselling cannot give Alex more time, which is what she would really like, but it might just help her to fully see the value and meaning that is already latent in her life and to make the most of her remaining days.

The type of philosophical counselling outlined above can perhaps best be described as an open-ended philosophical enquiry, which is the model of PC proposed by its founder Gerd Achenbach. But many philosophical counsellors have proposed semi-structured models of PC instead. Perhaps the most famous is Marinoff's PEACE model (Marinoff, 1999). In this book we will be looking at several methods which help clients with decision-making (Progress), values clarification and development (RSVP) and with the rational justification of beliefs, decisions and values (the Charles Darwin method). These methods preserve the Socratic spirit in that they do not impose a worldview on the client, but instead use a *method* to bring out and allow useful reflection on the client's own worldview.[11] We will return to the debate over whether PC is most effective as an open-ended or semi-structured activity later.

Philosophical counsellors use similar philosophical methods to academic philosophers, except that rather than employing them on an abstract problem they apply them to a concrete issue in the client's life. A second important difference is that they use these methods in a joint enquiry with the client, rather than on their own. In Alex's case, conceptual analysis is carried out on 'death' to decide whether it is a state or non-existence. Critical thinking is used to question the idea that immortality would be such a good thing; this analysis being aided by a Kantian thought experiment. The counsellor throughout would aim to be phenomenological in staying with Alex's concerns and meaning-system rather than merely informing her about philosophical ideas. The dialogue would touch on a variety of topics of philosophical interest, including death, the meaning of life, and well-being. Philosophical theories are brought in, including ancient ideas from Epicurus and Lucretius, ideas from Kant and the more modern thoughts of Robinson, Nagel and Williams. Note that these ideas are all treated as potential wisdom rather than as the 'wisdom of the ages' to be taken as the final authority. In this way PC captures the full spirit of philosophy – at its best, PC is a collaborative philosophical enquiry which also enhances the well-being of the client.

Cognitive behavioural therapy (CBT) and rational emotive behavioural therapy (REBT)[12]

CBT is a therapy originated by Aaron Beck in the 1950s which now enjoys very wide popularity (e.g. in the National Health Service in the UK) and claims impressive results, particularly for specific disorders such as phobias, anxiety and depression. Its philosophical origins are normally attributed to the Stoics, in particular Epictetus' view that 'Men are moved not by things but by their interpretations.' Cognitive therapists have developed a technology for identifying and correcting distortions in thinking which adversely affect our interpretations of events (see pp. 98–102). CBT is philosophical therefore not only in its Stoic roots but also in its attempt to teach clients how to avoid fallacies in critical thinking. Rational Emotive Behaviour Therapy (REBT), a form of cognitive therapy associated with Albert Ellis, advertises its philosophical roots most loudly. REBT differs from CBT in that while CBT emphasizes distortions in the inferences people make about factual statements (e.g. 'I will never get a job'), REBT focuses more on the irrationality of the evaluations that the client makes (e.g. 'It's awful that I will never get a job'). REBT equates well-being with happiness and asserts that evaluations that are inconsistent with happiness are irrational. REBT therefore combines neo-Stoic theories about emotional self-control with hedonistic neo-Epicurean ideas about value.

Existential–phenomenological counselling (EC)

Existential–phenomenological counselling (EC) is a form of psychotherapy which aims at enhancing clients' self-knowledge and allows them to be the author of their own lives. Its philosophical roots are to be found in the works of Heidegger, Sartre, Kierkegaard and other existentialist thinkers as well as Husserl and phenomenologists. Historically, EC began when Binswanger attempted to use Heidegger's theory therapeutically, an approach that was adapted by Rollo May and others in the United States. More recently its leading exponents have included Emmy van Deurzen and Ernesto Spinelli in the UK and Irvin Yalom in the USA. According to van Deurzen (1990) the goals of existential therapy include 'widening client's perspective on themselves and the world around them' and 'helping them find clarity on how to proceed in the future while taking lessons from the past and creating something valuable to live for in the present'. Spinelli (1989) puts it this way: 'the aim . . . is to offer the means for individuals to examine, confront and clarify and reassess their understanding of life, the problems encountered throughout their life, and the limits imposed upon the possibilities inherent in being-in-the-world'. Yalom (1989) clarifies what he sees as the four main limitations of being-in-the-world: 'I have found that four givens [of existence] that are particularly relevant to psychotherapy are the inevitability of death for each of us and for those we love, the freedom to make our lives as we will, our ultimate aloneness and the absence of any obvious meaning or sense to life.'

Most existential therapists agree that therapy proceeds phe-
nomenologically by attempting to be with the client and
understand their way of being-in-the-world. The therapist is a
facilitator rather than a teacher. This may make EC sound like
humanistic counselling, but whereas the latter has an optimistic
faith that the three 'core conditions' of empathy, congruence
and unconditional positive regard will lead to client growth, EC
has no such comforting messages. The therapist cultivates an
attitude of neutrality rather than unconditional positive regard
(Spinelli, 1989), helps the client enquire into meaning and
explore their personal worldview (van Deurzen-Smith, 1990)
and face the givens of human existence suggested by existentialist philosophers (Yalom, 1989).

Logotherapy

Logotherapy is sometimes classified as a form of existential
therapy, but in practice it is so different from EC that it is best
dealt with separately. Logotherapy is closely connected with the
theories and practice of one man, its inventor Viktor Frankl.
'This was the lesson I had to learn in three years spent in
Auschwitz and Dachau: other things being equal, those apt to
survive the camps were those oriented toward the future –
toward a task, or a person, waiting for them in the future, toward
a meaning to be fulfilled by them in the future' wrote Frankl in
The Unheard Cry for Meaning (1985), one of many best-sellers
which put logotherapy on the therapeutic map. Frankl attrib-
utes his own survival in the camps to his desire to write about the
importance of meaning. Frankl theorized that psychiatrists
should add a spiritual (or, more technically, *noetic*) side to
mankind to existing physical and psychological dimensions. In
fact Frankl argued that mankind has a 'will to meaning' stronger
than a will to pleasure, power or wealth. If mankind's will to
meaning is frustrated, people suffer from 'noogenic' neuroses
which, according to Frankl, account for 20 per cent of all neuroses. Logotherapists argue that the creation of meaning can

both remove symptoms and prevent their re-emergence, for example in cases of addiction, depression and attempted suicide. Furthermore, logotherapists see themselves as providing education toward each of us assuming responsibility for our lives. As Frankl writes, 'Man should not ask what he expects from life, but should rather understand that life expects something from him.' Last but certainly not least, logotherapy provides for an orientation toward meaning and values (Crumbaugh, 1973).

Although each of these approaches can certainly be described as philosophical, there has been surprisingly little attempt to compare them and examine how they can inform each other. Constructively exploring what each has to offer is one of the main aims of this book. This is a particularly promising project once one realizes that each approach harnesses some but not all of the philosophical methods described above. The cognitive therapies have developed a way of using critical thinking to help individuals toward more rational beliefs and emotions. Existential–phenomenological therapists use phenomenology as one of the methods to help the clients explore their value system. Logotherapists use creative thinking to help clients gain meaning. Philosophical counsellors, more than the other therapies, use conceptual analysis and the discussion of the ideas of the great philosophers. A prospect that excites me, which I ask readers to keep an open mind about, is that a really wise therapy might combine aspects of each; we will be making first, tentative steps toward seeing what an integrated philosophical approach to counselling would be like. Such a therapy must have sound foundations: nothing less than acceptable philosophical ideas about each of the philosophical topics. This sets the agenda for our project. Each of the next four chapters focuses on one of the philosophical topics: well-being, right and wrong, the emotions and reason, and the meaning of life. For each topic, we begin by examining philosophical theories and attempting to integrate them into an acceptable theory. We then use this theory to evaluate the various philosophical therapies, and from the acceptable elements of these construct a valuable way of working with clients. The fruits of this enterprise are pulled together in Chapter 6, which describes the resulting ideas and methods which will help clients towards wisdom in each of the areas covered – well-being and values, decision-making and right and wrong, reason and the emotions, and meaning in life.

How to use this book

Each chapter focuses on one topic, so it is quite possible for the reader interested only in well-being, for example, to read just that chapter. Similarly, prudent use of the index will enable the reader interested, in, say, only the insights and critique of exis-tential–phenomenological counselling to home in on those. Finally, those interested mainly in practical methods may wish to turn straight to Chapter 6: 'The Counsellor's Philosophical Toolbox'. However, the best way to read the book is in the normal manner, starting at the beginning. This is partly because of connections between the various topics – for example, right and wrong depends partly on well-being. Moreover, the book as a whole forms an argument. The methods of the 'Toolbox' are not plucked out of thin air but come from a consideration of the philosophical and therapeutic ideas discussed in the book.

This book is intended mainly for counsellors interested in how philosophy can help them. Obviously, one book cannot cover the whole of philosophy, and readers are referred to the 'Recommended Reading' and 'Resources' sections at the end of the book for further information and other viewpoints. Philo-sophical controversies which do not bear directly on the issues discussed in the book have been relegated to the 'Notes' section or omitted altogether; the interested reader is recommended to the Bibliography to pursue these further.

Although the subtitle of the book is 'Philosophy for Coun-sellors', I hope the book is also of interest to philosophers without a background in counselling. They should be warned, however, that this book does *not* tell the reader how to do counselling, and those without previous experience in counselling are strongly recommended to undertake a professional course in counselling skills before using the methods described in this book on other people.

I would be delighted to receive feedback on the exercises in this book, and indeed other comments. I can be reached by e-mail at timlebon@aol.com. Feedback, comments and updates will be posted on my website, http://members.aol.com/timlebon.

Part I
Ethics

From the dawn of philosophy, the question concerning the *summum bonum* [highest good], or, what is the same thing, concerning the foundation of morality, has been accounted the main problem of speculative thought. (J. S. Mill, *Utilitarianism*)

Counsellors need to consider the possibility of seriously investigating what life is all about and what people can do to live it better. (Emmy van Deurzen-Smith, *Can Counselling Help?*)

Introduction

For philosophers, ethics – the attempt to provide a reasoned account of well-being and right and wrong – is a key topic. To the counsellor and the practical philosopher, who are intimately concerned with the way people live and the decisions they make, ethics is absolutely central. Certainly ethics ought to be at the heart of counselling. *Every* approach to counselling is based on assumptions about what makes someone's life go well – be it autonomy, happiness, authenticity, rationality or self-actualization. Whether the goals of counselling are really as desirable as counselling theorists claim is a key question in the debate over whether counselling is a great good, worthy of public funding, or a potential evil. Consequently, counsellors need an overall theory of well-being in order to assess the benefits of their own paradigm. Also, all counsellors face ethical dilemmas in their own work, for example when they face decisions involving confidentiality or suicide. Counsellors need a practical method to help them deal with these issues which is consistent with acceptable philosophical theories about right and wrong. The ethical core of counselling is also apparent from the perspective of the client. Many clients – like Claire mentioned in Chapter 1 – come to counselling in a state of confusion over direction in life or facing difficult and complex decisions. How can the counsellor expect to help these clients make wise choices without an informed view of pertinent philosophical issues or a procedure which will help them think through these questions together with their clients? These concerns set the agenda for the next two chapters. The first part of our journey will be theoretical, with a brief excursion into metaethics and the foundations of ethics, before moving on to examine theories about well-being and right and wrong. We will then see exactly how philosophy can help clients to 'seriously investigate what life is all about' by looking at their own values – values-focused counselling. Next we investigate how best to construct a procedure to help counsellors make decisions about their own work, and to engage in decision counselling with their clients.

Metaethics: the foundations of ethics

We all face issues about which science says too little; theology too much. Philosophy provides a 'Middle Way.' (Lou Marinoff, 1998)

Metaethics is the branch of philosophy which discusses the foundations and status of ethics and can help us decide how best to proceed in our quest for ethical answers. As the well-known philosophical counsellor Lou Marinoff points out, two common approaches taken – an appeal to religion and to science – are not satisfactory.

Appeal to religion or authority

The religious might say that the good and the right are simply whatever is commanded by God, but this view is susceptible to the following argument, raised long ago by Plato. Plato's simple but devastating question – dubbed the 'Euthyphro question' after the dialogue in which it appears – is as follows:

> Is the good good because God commands it, or does God command it because it is good?

If *all* that can be said about the good is that God commands it, then the good is the product of an arbitrary will, and doing good is mere obedience to authority. An authority might, for example, say that killing is good – does that really make killing good?[1] This suggests that we should settle instead for the second possibility, that God commands us to do good things because they are *already* good, before God has passed his view. But this reply amounts to saying that it is not only God's will that makes something good. If God says that something is good because, for example, it leads to human happiness, then we don't actually need to know the divine will. We can try to work out directly what things lead to human happiness ourselves. So either way, an appeal to religion is not a satisfactory way to decide what is good or right.

The same argument applies to any appeal to authority, the law, or professional bodies which create codes of ethics and practice. Imagine the EAC (Evil Association for Counselling) which says that it's right to lie to clients, and embodies this rule in its Code of Ethics and Practice. As the argument of Euthyphro reminds us, it's not right to lie to clients *just* because the EAC tells us to. We must look at the reasons the EAC gives to justify its rule. As counsellors, we need to have a close look at the contents of Codes of Ethics and Practice before we sign up to them.

The 'Euthyphro question' does *not* mean that the source of ethical pronouncements is irrelevant, nor that we should disobey authorities. It does, however, mean that if we are trying to establish what is good and right, we have to find good reasons and arguments, independent of their source. Appeal to religion or other authority is not sufficient.

Appeal to science or to human nature

There are two senses in which science might be considered to say too little. First, there is no consensus about what human nature is, as evidenced by a recent book which describes as many as ten competing theories of human nature, one of which (Sartre's) denies that there even is such a thing as human nature (Stevenson and Haberman, 1998). Second, those elements of human nature that nearly everyone does agree about – basic human needs such as eating and sleeping – are too few and insufficiently rich to provide a plausible view of human flourishing (Griffin, 1986). Science (including psychology) can provide some information which we can hope to use when deciding the ingredients of well-being – for example, it can tell us how to cure disease, and it might well have useful things to say about how to be happy. But it cannot tell us how to decide whether health or happiness or something else actually are the main components of the good life. Science may be helpful, but it cannot say enough.

Philosophy's middle way

Philosophy's middle way consists in appealing neither to authority nor to science, but to the methods of philosophy introduced in Chapter 1. The rest of this book, in particular Chapters 2, 3 and 6, are illustrations of how we can make headway in ethics. Some readers may be reluctant to embark on this journey, thinking that if religion and science cannot deliver the goods, then philosophy is unlikely to either. In particular, they may think that well-being and right and wrong are just a matter of personal belief or feeling. If this were the case, then philosophy would not have much to contribute, and the best way for Claire and everyone else to proceed would be by consulting their beliefs or feelings. But these sceptical views are best dealt with by considering two philosophical theories which challenge philosophy's ability to help us sort out ethics. These two theories are relativism and emotivism.

Relativism[2]

Relativism is the view that there are no absolutes in ethics. One type of relativism, cultural relativism, points to the existence of different ethical practices in different societies and asserts that there is no overarching position from which we can judge these practices. Eating dog is right in Korea, eating pig is right in the West. No more can be said about the matter. Another version of relativism says that ethics is relative to the individual. Fred may think that there are occasions when it is right to break confidentiality in counselling, Joan thinks that it is never right. This sort of relativist says that this is purely a matter of personal belief.

Emotivism

Emotivism is the theory that ethical statements are just the expression of the speaker's emotions or attitude. If I say to you 'Counselling should be available as part of free health care', I am just expressing my emotions, like someone who says 'Come on you reds' in support of a football team. I am, according to the emotivist, saying 'Hurray for free counselling' – hence emotivism's nickname of the 'Boo-Hurray theory of ethics'.

Both theories contain important insights. In the first place they remind us that ethical statements do not appear to be simple or straightforward[3] statements of objective fact. The statement 'Therapy is good' is not an objective statement of fact such as 'The sky is blue'. In general, facts are established by appeal to one of our five senses. Sight informs us that the sky is blue. What is the corresponding sense which informs us that therapy is good? If Freud says that therapy is good, but critics think it bad, what sense can tell us which view is correct?

But both theories seriously overstate their case.[4] It's not true, as relativists think, that there are no commonly held values among societies or individuals. For instance, do those attracted to relativism really think it's just their opinion that the atrocities committed in Hitler's Germany were wrong? The fact that ethical practices differ should be taken as a challenge to us to investigate and justify our own moral intuitions rather than an indication that all moral practices are equally right. Emotivism is correct in stressing that ethical statements are connected with emotions and attitudes, but it forgets that attitudes and emotions themselves are not just a case of saying 'Hurray!' but themselves involve evaluations.[5]

If Freud says 'Therapy is good', it would be entirely appropriate (if a little impractical) to ask him for reasons to back up his statement. Ethical statements differ in this respect from arbitrary tastes, such as my liking for Tottenham Hotspur football team, which I may have no inclination to defend (especially at the time of writing). If I say 'I like Tottenham' I don't have to give a reason for it: it's just a blind preference. If instead I had said 'Supporting Tottenham is right', I would be going beyond saying that I like them, suggesting that they are worthy of being liked. Then I could be expected to give reasons for this view.[6]

We can see this if we return to Graham, Susan's smug anti-therapy psychiatrist friend of Chapter 1. Recall Graham's pronouncement that 'Empirical studies show that counselling is a cost-ineffective way of helping people, and it would be quite wrong to provide public money to subsidize it.' Of course Graham's statement is a personal belief, and it is also an expression of his feelings – but it is more than this. Graham has given a reason for saying that counselling is cost-ineffective – the evidence of empirical studies. The first step in disputing Graham's assertion would be to examine these empirical studies, to see exactly what they do show. To generalize, behind any ethical claim there are factual statements which can be disputed and, often, resolved. For example, Susan might find contradictory studies, or she might find that Graham's or the studies' criteria for 'helping people' are too narrow.

These points are sufficient to show that ethics is not just a matter of personal belief or an expression of feelings. It might be thought that this might sort out ethics. All we have to do, it might be thought, is to examine the reasons for and against each position and use the tools of critical thinking to decide which case is the stronger. But sometimes this seems not to end the matter. Graham and Susan may agree on the facts but disagree about what they mean by 'helping' and 'wrong'. For example, it may turn out that the evidence shows that counselling is indeed not a cost-effective way of *removing the symptoms* of depression compared to medication, but that counselling, unlike medication, allows the client an opportunity for self-understanding. Graham and Susan may disagree about whether self-understanding helps people and whether it is right to subsidize a process that facilitates self-understanding. If this is the case, then only an elucidation of 'well-being' and 'right and wrong' will allow further progress in the dispute.

Philosophical tools like conceptual analysis and critical thinking can certainly be helpful in progressing ethical disputes, for example by looking at the evidence for underlying factual assumptions. But they will be more helpful still if we have a good understanding of the key concepts of 'well-being' and 'right and wrong'. This sets the agenda for the next two chapters. Chapter 2 explores philosophical theories of well-being, Chapter 3 right and wrong. Our aim will be to not only to get a better theoretical understanding but also to develop practical methods which will allow us to explore how to enhance an individual's well-being and to make good decisions.

2 | Well-being

Philosophical theories of well-being

According to *hedonism* (the first theory of well-being we will consider), well-being consists in having pleasant and desirable experiences. The second theory, the *objective value* theory, sees this as too subjective. According to this view, well-being isn't necessarily a matter of doing pleasant things: it's more a case of fulfilling certain values which hold objectively for all humans, no matter what particular individuals want or think. The final theory – *the informed preference theory* – posits that well-being is getting what you would want if you were fully informed and rational. This view lies somewhere between hedonism and objective theories. It allows for a richer and more objective account of the good life than hedonism, but still sees a link between what people want and what is good that is lacking in objective value theories.

Hedonism[1]

> Nature has placed mankind under the governance of two sovereign masters, pain and pleasure. It is for them alone to point out what we ought to do, as well as determine what we shall do.
> (Bentham, 1948)

The nineteenth-century philosopher and reformer Jeremy Bentham held that well-being is pleasure and the absence of pain (or, sometimes and without concern for the difference, happiness and the absence of unhappiness). This theory, hedonism, has been advocated by philosophical notables such as Epicurus, Hobbes and Hume and in counselling has greatly influenced REBT and, to a lesser extent, CBT. Sophisticated forms of hedonism stated in terms of happiness are much more plausible than crude versions formulated in terms of pleasure. Happiness can be equated with all positive states of mind, including emotional episodes such as feeling elated or proud and longer-lasting states such as feelings of achievement and autonomy, as well as pleasure. Hedonism has the considerable virtue that it tells us to think of our long-term rather than short-term happiness, reminding us to forgo present pleasures if they would lead to great pains in the future and to put up with present frustrations if there is the promise of future happiness.

But is happiness the only thing that matters? There's little doubt that, other things being equal, happiness and the absence of unhappiness are good. But are they the only thing that's good? The contemporary Oxford philosopher James Griffin thinks not. He distinguishes two potential components of well-being, *states of mind* and *states of the world* (Griffin, 1986). A 'state of the world' is the objective, actual state of affairs, which may well be different from what an individual takes to be the case.[2] Hedonism's claim that states of mind are the only good thing is cast into doubt when we consider situations where one is in a positive state of mind but is ignorant or deluded about the real state of the world. One such situation is that suggested by the 'Experience Machine'.

The 'Experience Machine'
The American philosopher Robert Nozick asks us to imagine an 'Experience Machine' that enables you to experience whatever state of mind you choose (Nozick, 1974). Plug yourself into the machine and you need never feel pain again. Instead you could feel perfect pleasure, or pride at painting the Mona Lisa, or elation at winning an Olympic gold – the choice is yours. And

while you are plugged in to the machine, *you will not be aware of being plugged in.* If hedonists are right, then surely everyone would choose to be wired to the machine. Would you choose to be plugged in?

Some people respond that they would not, because they doubt whether the machine would work, or worry that their body would not be attended to, or they say that being in the machine would get boring after a while. All these objections can be overcome. The machine is guaranteed to work, a team of people will care for your body, and the machine will produce whatever sequence of states of mind you most prefer. It could even be programmed to give you the optimum level of frustration so that you are deliriously happy when things turn out well. The soccer supporter will find their team 2–0 down with five minutes to go – and be ecstatic and surprised each time they score three times in the last five minutes. But even after being given these reassurances, most people stop short of wanting to spend their life in the machine. A few hours would be fun, but a lifetime – no way. It is enlightening to consider why the Experience Machine is not most people's answer to well-being. There are various things wrong with life in the Experience Machine. Life would, in a sense, be meaningless, and we would lack autonomy. But I believe that the most fundamental thing wrong is that we do not make a difference to the world. We may *think* that we are painting the Mona Lisa, or eradicating famine in Africa, but in fact we are sitting in a laboratory plugged in to the machine, doing nothing. Our reaction to the possibility of being plugged in to the Experience Machine highlights a general flaw in hedonism: the hedonist fails to take into account the importance of actual states of the world. For this reason hedonism has other unacceptable implications, such as falsely suggesting that we cannot be harmed by something we never find out about (for example, someone reading our private mail). A more satisfactory account must recognize that states of the world are important, as well as states of mind.[3]

Objective value theories[4]

> The true lover of knowledge naturally strives for truth, and is
> not content with common opinion, but soars with undimmed and
> unwearied passion till he grasps the essential nature of things.
> (Plato, *The Republic*, 490A)

Objective value theories assert that well-being consists in our
lives coming up to an objective standard of the good life. This
theory perhaps most closely matches the commonsense view,
and that held by religion, that we need to be told what to do precisely because doing what is pleasant or doing what we want
might not be best for us. As it stands, the objective value theory
does not give us any practical help – what we need is a list of
values, things that ought to be pursued as ingredients of a good
life. Different philosophers have suggested different values.
Here are some of them:[5]

> Accomplishment, autonomy, liberty, health, understanding, enjoy-
> ment and deep personal relations. (Griffin, 1986)

> Life, knowledge, play, aesthetic experience, friendship, practical
> reasonableness and religion. (Finnis, 1980)

> Life, beauty, truth, reason and love. (Robinson, 1964)

Difficulties with the objective value theory of well-being

The idea that values are objective is attractive to many people. It
fits in with our intuition, confirmed by the Experience Machine
thought experiment, that states of mind are not the only things
that matter. But the objective theory faces three serious objections.

1. *How does the theory take into account cultural and individual differences?*

   Why should we expect one set of values to lead to the flourishing of all human beings, of each gender, in all cultures, at all stages of their life? Recall that we have argued that well-being consists in both a good state of mind and a good state of the world. Even if states of the world may be objectively good or bad, it's harder to see why everyone should find that the same things always lead to preferred states of mind. For example, the acquisition of knowledge may for some people be a very stimulating experience; for others it may be drudgery. We should, according to this objection, be open to the possibility that different people may have different values.

2. *What sort of things are 'objective values'?*

   We have already noted (p. 25) that moral statements such as 'Therapy is good' are not straightforward factual statements like 'The sky is blue'. The twentieth-century Oxford philosopher J. L. Mackie has argued that although many talk as if values are part of the material furniture of the world, they are mistaken. The title of his book, *Ethics: Inventing Right and Wrong*, states his position concisely (Mackie, 1977). 'Objective values ... would', says Mackie, 'be entities or qualities or relations of a very strange sort, utterly different from anything else in the universe.' Mackie's objection is at its most persuasive when aimed at the most famous objective theory of all – that advanced by Plato in *The Republic*, according to which values are unchanging, eternally existing entities, existing outside time and space.[6]

3. *How do we gain our knowledge of values?*

   None of the five senses appear to give us knowledge of values, and appeals to authority and to human nature have also been dismissed as inadequate. Griffin, Finnis and Robinson have provided us with three different lists of values (see p. 31), with some overlap but plenty of divergence. Since they cannot all be right, the obvious question is – how does one decide which is right?

Discussion

None of these points prove that values cannot be objective. They are best seen as putting up three 'hurdles' which any satisfactory objective theory must negotiate:

1. It must either allow for or explain apparent individual differences in values, and value states of mind as well as states of the world.
2. It must not depend on totally mysterious entities like Plato's Forms.
3. It must tell us how we gain our knowledge of values, and allow us to distinguish acceptable values from unacceptable ones.

The satisfaction of informed preferences (IPT)

> The ultimate criterion of what constitutes human well-being is whatever would be preferred by people whose choices were not constrained by ignorance or irrationality. (Holmes and Lindley, 1991)

We need a theory which builds on what is acceptable in hedonism and objective theories but avoids their errors. The informed preference theory (IPT) sees well-being as consisting in whatever people would choose if not constrained by ignorance or irrationality. It is an attractive theory. Hedonism's fatal flaw – that it ignores actual states of the world – is avoided because IPT says that well-being depends on our preferences being satisfied, not merely us *thinking* that they are satisfied. Neither does IPT require the existence of any mysterious entities. Objectivity is obtained by preferences being well-informed and rational. IPT also seems right in that it recognizes individual differences, another potential problem for objective theories. If you like tomatoes and I don't, IPT takes our preferences into account and allows that tomatoes may be good for you but bad for me. IPT is such a promising theory because it combines the following three ingredients.

The satisfaction of human preferences

Any theory of well-being which has no connection with human wants should be rejected. Imagine if someone claimed to have invented a 'Well-being Machine', promising you well-being at the touch of a button. Intrigued, you press the button, only to find out that it turns everything yellow. You complain, but the inventor assures you that well-being consists in everything being yellow. 'But I don't want everything to be yellow!', you reply. Heaven is thought desirable only because it contains things that we want – like eternal bliss and the absence of pain. If we were told that heaven does not contain things we actually want, or would want once we had them, then we would no longer find it attractive.

Preferences should be informed

Other things being equal, getting what we want is a good thing: but 'other things' are not always equal. Our preferences are not always well-informed, and in these cases satisfying them does not enhance our well-being. Freda wants to get on a train because she thinks it goes to her home in North London, but it's really the Glasgow Express. All his life Frank has wanted to live in the country but when he finally achieves this he is miserable because he had not appreciated how isolated he would feel. Philip values chastity because he believes that God demands it, but it may turn out that God does not demand chastity, or even that God does not exist.

It is helpful to distinguish between those things that we want just because they lead to something else we want ('instrumental preferences') and things that we want for their own sake ('ultimate values'[7] or sometimes just 'values'). Freda's getting on a train because she wants to get home is an instrumental preference – she does not want to get on the train for any other reason than that it will get her home. Philip's chastity is an ultimate value; he is not chaste for its consequences, but because he thinks that it is right.

It is important to see that both instrumental preferences and ultimate values need to be well informed. It's easy to see this with instrumental preferences – if we are misinformed about what they lead to, then we will no longer want them. It's less obvious that ultimate values can be misinformed and quite tempting to think that, because they are ultimate, they are blind choices. However, there are two ways in which even ultimate values can be misinformed. Ultimate values are in fact not arbitrary but are held for reasons which can be said to be the *presuppositions* of the values (Kekes, 1992). Philip's chastity would be misinformed if God does not demand chastity or if God does not exist. Furthermore, if we have a plurality of ultimate values then the satisfaction of one can have an impact on the satisfaction of the others. Philip's chastity has an impact on the satisfaction of his pleasure. Philip might come to realize that pleasure is actually more important than chastity, and that he should actually, on balance, consider chastity to be a disvalue.

Preferences should be rational[8]

Imagine that you are giving your baby a bath, and it starts screaming loudly and uncontrollably. You find yourself with a sudden and strong desire to drown it. Should you? Clearly not, and this suggests a third requirement for preferences, namely that they be rational. The contemporary philosopher Michael Smith uses this example to argue that we should aim for the satisfaction of preferences which we would keep if we were reflecting under idealized conditions of being well informed, cool, calm and collected (Smith, 1994). Smith gives us the conditions for reflections; the way we should reflect on each of our desires and preferences is partially suggested by a very old Epicurean idea. The following method of inquiry must be applied to every desire: What will happen to me if what I long for is accomplished? What will happen if it is not accomplished? (Epicurus, *Vatican Sayings,* 71, discussed in de Botton, 2000).

We should try to satisfy only those preferences and desires which we would accept as a good reason for action when reflecting in this way. We need to think about what our state of mind and the state of the world would really be like if each desire was fulfilled. Furthermore, the *strength* of the preference should match the strength that it would have when we reflect in this way. A preference, for example to paint a perfect picture, may become irrational only when its strength is such that it overrides other preferences (such as those for having a break to eat). We should also consider our *future* preferences as well as our current ones. Imagine that Jim is 25 and leading a happy and satisfying life. When he was 18 he had a series of overwhelming personal crises, which led to him contemplating suicide. At the time, he could see no reason to carry on living. However, aged 25 he is extremely glad that he did not commit suicide at 18. It was rational for him to take into account the possibility that his future preferences when older might differ from his current ones.

It might seem at this stage that we have moved a long way from equating well-being with the satisfaction of actual preferences. Should we agree with Nicholas Rescher that 'The genuinely rational person is the one who proceeds in situations of choice by asking himself not the introspective question "What do I prefer?" but the objective question "What is to be deemed preferable? What ought I to prefer?"' (Rescher, 1988). No, because Rescher is proposing a false polarization. It is not a case of *either* looking at what we prefer *or* what we ought to prefer: what we need to do is first look at what we prefer, then what we would prefer in ideal conditions, and finally infer what we ought to prefer.

Conclusion

I believe that the informed preference theory provides a convincing account of human well-being. It clearly is an improvement on hedonism, because it recognizes value in both states of mind and states of the world. It also has claims to objectivity in that preferences must be both well informed and rational. In fact, there is a good case for saying that it passes the three hurdles we said that any plausible objective theory must pass, and is itself an acceptable objective theory about well-being.[9] It allows for differences in values – we have not legislated that the informed and rational Chelsea pensioner and a Nepalese herdsman will have the same ultimate values (although they might). IPT is also immune from Mackie's objection. There is nothing mysterious about ultimate values: they are just statements about what we would want under certain ideal conditions. Finally, we know how to distinguish acceptable values from unacceptable ones. Acceptable values are those which, we would agree, have acceptable presuppositions and consequences when reflecting in the prescribed manner under ideal conditions.

Can counselling help?

Having found an acceptable account of well-being, we will now examine its practical implications for counselling, which as we shall see are quite considerable. We will begin by examining autonomy, commonly forwarded as the rationale of counselling, in the light of this analysis, and then move on to see what a wise therapy constructed to produce enlightened values would be like.

Autonomy as the aim of counselling

Holmes and Lindley (1991, p. 52) are surely right in claiming that enhancing autonomy is 'a common theme in the overwhelming majority of therapies'. However, different theorists mean different things by autonomy. There are two main meanings:

1. Autonomy as the opportunity to implement one's own choices.
2. Autonomy as the opportunity to implement one's own informed and rational choices.

The first meaning, which equates autonomy with doing what one wants, is probably the most common usage in counselling. Yet people can be ill-informed and irrational – and if they are, what is the value of encouraging them to implement their own choices? As Charles Taylor has argued:

> [There is] a general presumption of subjectivism about value: things have significance not of themselves but because people deem them to have it – as though people could determine what is significant, either by decision, or perhaps unwittingly and unwillingly just by feeling that way. This is crazy. I couldn't just *decide* that the most significant action is wiggling my toes in warm mud.
>
> But if it makes sense only with an explanation (perhaps mud is the element of the world spirit, which you contact with your toes), it is open to criticism. What if the explanation is wrong, doesn't pan out, or can be replaced with a better account? Your feeling a certain way can never be sufficient grounds for respecting your position, because your feeling can't *determine* what is significant. Soft relativism self-destructs. (Taylor, 1991, pp. 36–7)

Taylor is surely right in suggesting that mere decisions or feelings cannot of themselves determine what is of value. Decisions and feelings, like preferences, can be ill-informed and irrational.[10] Consider the case of Ivan Ilyich, described in Tolstoy's classic short story *The Death of Ivan Ilyich*. On his deathbed Ivan, a wealthy and successful man, suddenly realizes that he has been wrong all his life about what matters. He now deeply regrets squandering his life in superficial material pursuits without doing the things that he now realizes were really important. Ivan had always been fully autonomous, in the first sense – his problem was that his values had been neither informed nor rational. If counselling is to adopt autonomy as a core value, it should be in the second sense. This may seem to go against one of counselling's most sacred rules, which is that the counsellor should respect the client's values. However, many implicitly equate 'having respect' with 'unwisely colluding with any apparent value the client has got hold of'. Ivan Ilyich and others like him are hardly respected by letting them continue to live by values which they themselves would not agree with had they thought them through more.

Counselling's hidden potential

Emmy van Deurzen-Smith (1994) has argued that although counselling can help, it has not fulfilled its hidden potential, something it will do only when it takes its role as applied philosophy more seriously. There are three important ways in which counselling can help people achieve true autonomy through applied philosophy: towards enlightened values, good decisions and emotional wisdom. Exploring how philosophy can do this sets a large part of this book's agenda. In this chapter, we look at how counselling can help clients have more enlightened values, in the next chapter how it can help them make good decisions, and in the following one how clients can be helped move towards emotional wisdom.

Values-focused counselling

One of the most important ways that counselling can help is by enabling people to figure out in what their well-being consists. Our earlier discussion suggests that the informed preference theory (IPT) provides an acceptable general framework to help people do this. Michael Smith says that rational values are those that we would accept when reflecting under idealized conditions which include being well informed, cool, calm and collected. My suggestion is that the counselling room provides the perfect arena for such reflection, and applied philosophy the perfect tool. Reflection will focus on *ultimate values* – those things that people think make their lives worth living, both in terms of positive states of mind and states of the world. It will consist of two phases – a creative phase of trying to think up significant ultimate values, and a critical phase of deciding which of these values are most acceptable. This – the RSVP procedure – is our final destination. But before arriving there, we need to look at existing, philosophically inspired modes of counselling to see if they can provide techniques that can be readily used in our aim of doing what I call 'Values-focused counselling'. The approaches we will be examining are logotherapy, existential–phenomenological counselling (EC) and philosophical counselling (PC).

Logotherapy

Logotherapy's focus on meaning inevitably leads it also to say a good deal about values. James Crumbaugh (1973) has suggested that meaning can be gained through the satisfaction of three sorts of values – creative, experiential and attitudinal. Creative values encapsulate not only things we create and achieve but also how we affect other people. But we value not only things that we create, but also things that we experience. As Frankl (1965) writes, 'Let us ask a mountain-climber who has beheld the alpine sunset and is so moved by the splendour of nature that he feels cold shudders running down his spine – let us ask him whether after such an experience his life can ever again seem wholly meaningless.' Reading a story or spending an hour in the arms of one's beloved are other examples of experiential values. Finally, meaning and value can be attained not only by *what* we create or experience, but by *how* we interpret it. Our attitude can completely change the meaning and value of an event. Frankl argues that we always have the freedom to find meaning through our attitudes even in apparently meaningless situations. For example, an elderly, depressed patient who could not overcome the loss of his wife was helped by the following conversation (Frankl, 1959). Frankl asked 'What would have happened if you had died first, and your wife would have had to survive you?' 'Oh', replied the patient, 'for her this would have been terrible; how she would have suffered!' Frankl continued, 'You see such a suffering has been spared her; and it is you who have spared her this suffering; but now, you have to pay for it by surviving her and mourning her.' The man said no word, but shook Frankl's hand and calmly left his office.

As we have already noted, most texts on logotherapy talk a lot about meaning and values, but say very little about how they can actually be enhanced. Crumbaugh's great contribution is to provide a series of exercises which he gives to clients to help them enhance meaning in their life. Here is a sample of what Crumbaugh calls his 'exercises of logoanalysis' (Figure 2.1).[11]

The question we need to ask is – to what extent would Crumbaugh's clients be helped to develop enlightened values? I believe that many clients would be helped considerably. We can see this if we examine his three categories in terms of states of

---

1. Meaning through creative values

a) What would your epitaph be?
b) What would you give as a reason for continuing to live if a murderer asked you for a reason to be spared?

For each of the above:

i)   What are the underlying needs and values?
ii) How could you fulfil the underlying values?

2. Meaning through experiential values

Consider examples from art, nature and science (e.g. a story, a beautiful landscape) and record what meaning they suggest.

3. Meaning through attitudinal values

Consider how you handled an episode in your life. What purpose could there have been in the event? Could you have adopted a different attitude that would have helped you?

Figure 2.1   Crumbaugh's exercises of logoanalysis.
            Source: Crumbaugh (1973).

mind and states of the world. Creative values help us focus on how we can make a difference to the world. In thinking of an epitaph, we are trying to sum up how we would like to be remembered as part of the world. For example, 'I would like to be remembered as a good friend' highlights value with respect to other people. An answer of 'Because my children need me' would reveal that one's children's welfare was an underlying value. Experiential values fairly obviously focus on experiences and states of mind, the other component of well-being. For example, a commuter might answer 'The view of Westminster from the top of the bus as I ride over Waterloo Bridge.' This suggests that beauty is a value and provides meaning. Attitudinal values are perhaps most interesting of all, because they suggest that our state of mind can be positive almost regardless of the actual state of the world, a message the Stoics would endorse. They also remind us that well-being does not just consist in trying to satisfy ultimate values in the future; it also consists in a feeling of acceptance of the past. For example, a failed job interview could be interpreted as having the positive purpose of telling us that we really are not suited to do the job in question, or perhaps it just tells us we need to work harder at our interview technique; either way we need not view the event as an indictment of our future prospects. Crumbaugh's exercises are particularly useful in the task of creatively thinking up values; they are less use in deciding whether these values really are enlightened.

Existential–phenomenological counselling (EC)

Existentialism has a curiously ambivalent attitude to values and well-being. On the one hand, existentialist writers have been strongly critical of those who merely follow the 'herd' in blindly accepting the values of society. But many existentialists would probably resist the conclusion drawn in the preceding section, that some values can be more informed, rational or enlightened than others. This is somewhat strange, because if some values cannot be superior to others, it is hard to see why one should not merely follow the herd after all.[12] This ambivalence of existentialist philosophers is reflected in the practice of some existential counsellors, who do not see their work as focusing on values at all, but rather as helping the client explore and get another perspective on whatever material they bring up. Nevertheless, EC does provide us with two potential methods for helping clients towards enlightened values.

1. Emotions as the royal road to values

It was earlier stated that none of the five senses directly detect value. Without going back on this, I would like to consider the view that we have a sixth sense – the emotions – which can play this role and be, in my colleague David Arnaud's apt phrase, the 'royal road to values' (Arnaud and LeBon, 2000). A contemporary American philosopher, Joel Kupperman (Kupperman, 1999), has argued that emotions are very much like a sense which helps us detect value. Kupperman identifies admiration and despising as the two emotions most helpful in values clarification. Other emotions, such as envy, respect (and its absence), anger and love may also indicate what is of value to us. In counselling we can help people focus on their values either by asking them about whom they admire, envy, respect and feel passionate about – or else we can just wait for them to express these emotions and point out their implications. For example, if Jo, a frustrated musician, says that she can't see any value in her life, but at the same time is very passionate about her music, it could usefully be pointed out that she does have values, and these are to be found in her music; her problem is rather that these values are not, as yet, being sufficiently satisfied. We will further consider the role of emotions as the royal road to values, and as information in general, in Chapter 4. At this stage, though, we should point out that if emotions are to be considered as a sixth sense, they are not an altogether reliable one. We may, for example, find that we admire people who have been successful in their career, and deduce from this that success in a career is a value for us; but then, on investigation, realize that having a successful career does not have quite the favourable consequences one imagined. The emotions are better at telling us about our *senses of value* than what to actually value.

2. The four dimensions of existence (Binswanger and van Deurzen-Smith)

Binswanger originally identified three dimensions of existence as being the physical, psychological and public worlds, to which van Deurzen-Smith added a fourth dimension, the spiritual or ideal. Existential therapy aims to increase awareness of each dimension, and there is also the suggestion that people might benefit from harmony and balance between the dimensions. In values focused counselling we can ask clients about the values already implicit in their dealings with nature and their bodies, their emotions and intimate relations, and their jobs and status, and ask them to think about what a desirable balance between them would be.

Philosophical counselling (PC)

While some philosophical counsellors have argued that ethics and values should be at the heart of PC (e.g. Feary, quoted in Marinoff, 1999), most see PC as a much more open-ended enquiry, where neither the subject matter nor answers are decided in advance. There is something very attractive in the idea that, in Shlomit Schuster's (1999) words, PC is a 'free space' for the client to try to think through whatever seems to be of importance to them. It certainly captures the philosophical spirit mentioned in Chapter 1. Though valuable, this style of philosophical counselling suffers from two potential drawbacks. First, it has been suggested (e.g. by Shibles, 1998 and Scruton, 1997) that PC presupposes relativism, which, as we have seen, is not a very attractive theory. Though not entirely fair, one can see how this view could be arrived at. PC seems to suggest that we do not try to decide in advance which theory (say hedonism, or the objective theory, or IPT) is right. PC seems to involve either telling the client about whatever theory we think will be most helpful to them, regardless of its truth (Scruton, 1997) or else trying to facilitate them coming to their own views – which may be a very inefficient and unreliable way of proceeding, if some answers really are better than others.[13] Second, if the counsellor does not ensure that values are focused on, then they might never be focused on. PC that is not sufficiently directive in terms of method seems unduly optimistic regarding the client's knowledge about how best to use PC.

I believe that these criticisms are best overcome in two ways. Later I will describe the RSVP method, which is designed specifically to help people develop enlightened values, without imposing any values on them. For those philosophical counsellors who would like the enquiry to be more open-ended than this but would still like some focus, I propose the following alternative four-stage Socratic method to help clients lead 'the good life'.

Philosophical counselling and the good life – a Socratic method[14]

1. Asking for a provisional account of the good life

According to Plato's dialogues, Socrates usually began his quest for the examined life with a request for an account or definition of a key concept. Philosophical counselling has much in common with the Socratic approach, not least the notion that one is 'midwife' to the ideas of the client. Asking for such an account helps to make explicit the already implicit views they have about, in this case, what makes life go well. The answer given might range from a short, positive one (e.g. 'happiness') to a denial that there is an answer (e.g. 'It's impossible to say anything general about what makes life go well'). Either way, we could proceed to the next stage.

2. Testing the proposed account of 'the good life' philosophically

As in one of Plato's dialogues, this definition would now be the subject of a mutual enquiry. Both counsellor and client reflect on the validity of the account. Can we think of counter-examples? Are we clear about the meaning of the terms we have used? Is it meant to cover all people for all times? At this stage it is possible (but by no means necessary) to discuss the proposed account in the context of the ideas of academic philosophers; a collection I strongly recommend is Peter Singer's *Ethics: The Oxford Reader* (1994) which has an excellent section on 'Ultimate Good' comparing ideas from as varied thinkers as Buddha, Epictetus, Bentham, Mill, Camus and Parfit.

3. Testing the proposed account of 'the good life' against experience

The original account will very likely have been improved by applying the traditional tools of philosophical analysis to it, but we still would not know whether it fits with the client's own life experience. In order to discover this, the third stage looks at whether the proposed account can adequately explain variations in how they perceive their life has gone. Good philosophical counselling involves a fluid dialectic between each of these three stages, with the intention of arriving at an account which encompasses insights from both abstract analysis and life.

4. Helping put the accepted account of the good life into practice

If the first two stages are Socratic, aiming at *sophia* (intellectual wisdom), the final one is Aristotelian in that it is more concerned with *phronesis* (practical wisdom). For clients, as for Aristotle, it is important not only to know generally in what the good life consists, but to be able to apply this knowledge to particular cases. This stage might well involve a philosophical dialogue about what such practical wisdom consists in – for example, is it connected with perception of alternatives, or does it perhaps consist more in inculcating the right dispositions? Practical issues such as the barriers to the good life for this particular client and how to overcome them could also be touched on.

An example

How philosophical counselling could help one lead 'the examined life' might become clearer with an example. Suppose that a client, let's call her Sue, said that feeling happy is the key to the good life. This provisional account would be reflected upon, perhaps by asking Sue whether, like Bentham, she saw happiness as just quantities of pleasure or whether, like J. S. Mill, she thought it was better to be 'Socrates dissatisfied than a pig satisfied.' Such considerations might lead her to say that the good life consists in making choices which are not constrained by ignorance or irrationality. The next question would be whether her actual life could be construed in these terms. Did her life experience support the view that things went badly when she made ignorant or irrational choices? If it did, then the final stage would consider how she could make her future choices in a better informed and more rational way. What were her preferences now about what she should do, and had she sufficient information to make her choices? It should be clear that the fourth stage does not normally end in closure or certainty about what to do, but in a whole new set of questions. In this case they might include 'How much information and what sort of information do I need?' and 'Does this information include self-knowledge about the sort of person I am?' Philosophical counselling cannot of course guarantee that life will go well, but it surely helps one towards 'the examined life'. It might even have satisfied Socrates.

Developing enlightened values using RSVP

Each of these three philosophical forms of counselling – logotherapy, existential–phenomenological counselling and philosophical counselling – will all help people focus more on their well-being and their values. However, none of them quite gets to the bottom of helping them come up with an acceptable set of enlightened values which the informed preference theory suggests they need. Here I will describe a method (RSVP) which uses the insights of each of these theories and integrates them and other ideas implied by the informed preference theory.

RSVP has the following five steps.

1. Generating 'candidate' values.
2. Grouping values together.
3. Assessing whether each 'candidate' value should be accepted.
4. Clarifying the relative importance of each value.
5. Writing down virtues and goals associated with each value.

RSVP is described in detail in Chapter 6, and interested readers are strongly recommended to work through it for themselves on their own values. RSVP aims to develop enlightened values: by 'enlightened' I mean no more than those values which would stand the tests suggested by Smith and Epicurus of being accepted when cool, calm, collected and well informed. There are two ways that we can fail to have enlightened values: one is by not being creative enough to think up the values in the first place, and the other is by not being critical enough to accept and reject the right ones.

RSVP starts, in Stage 1 (generating candidate values), by doing a lot of creative thinking to come up with 'candidate' values, and then proceeds, in Stages 2 (grouping values together), 3 (assessing whether they should be accepted) and 4 (clarifying the relative importance of each value) to do critical thinking on each value. Finally, Stage 5 (working on associated virtues and goals) is concerned with helping to implement the values. At Stage 1, when we are doing our creative thinking, we use insights from logotherapy, existential–phenomenological counselling and philosophy to help us think of likely places from which enlightened values may come. For example, logotherapy tells us they might come from experiences, creations or attitudes (recall Crumbaugh's exercises on p. 41) and existential–phenomenological counselling suggests they might be placed in one of the four dimensions of existence and be detected by looking at certain emotions. Philosophy informs us to search for value in both states of mind and states of the world, and to use the Experience Machine and other thought experiments to help identify values. Stages 2, 3 and 4 use critical thinking (plus some conceptual analysis) to help work out whether these 'candidate' values should be accepted. It does this by looking at both the consequences of adopting them, the presuppositions they depend upon, and assessing whether the reasons for adopting the values are true, relevant and important. Finally, at Stage 5 we recognize that listing the values is not enough – we also need to work out virtues and goals that will help us live by them.

How to use RSVP

RSVP is presented in Chapter 6 in the style of a self-help exercise which might be given to clients. This is not intended to imply that it should necessarily be used in this way. First, it is very long, and its size might well be off-putting to clients. If used as an exercise for clients, I would certainly recommend splitting it up in to more manageable chunks. For example, the Life Review is a good exercise to give out on its own. However, its use is not limited to 'homework' exercises. It could easily inspire parts of the dialogue between counsellor and client – indeed many parts are intended to stimulate ideas and thought rather than come up with final answers. RSVP is best thought of as providing a framework to stimulate the client to think up and reflect upon their values, as much as a blueprint to produce the answers. Obviously experienced counsellors will also be sensitive to whether RSVP or its elements suit a particular client at a specific stage of counselling. For some clients either the complexities of their situation or their emotional state are more at issue than their value system.

Conclusion

Theories of well-being matter to counsellors for two reasons – to check that the aims of counselling (such as autonomy) are congruent with well-being, and to shape counselling so that it enhances well-being. We have seen how the informed preference theory can be developed in a way that makes it an acceptable theory and one with important implications for counsellors. It supports the idea that counsellors can enhance autonomy by helping clients develop enlightened values, rather than just satisfying the values with which they find themselves. Some existing counselling approaches – logotherapy, existential–phenomenological counselling and philosophical counselling – already contain some of the elements needed to enable counsellors to do value-focused counselling. We have shown how they can be integrated together, into a procedure like RSVP, to facilitate both the creative thinking up of values and the critical reflection on whether they really are enlightened.

3 | Right and Wrong

Dilemma 1: The suicidal client

Jan is a volunteer counsellor in her first year at a placement. From the first session her client, Judith, has talked about suicidal feelings. In the latest session, two months into therapy, Judith appears very depressed. It is fifteen minutes to the end of the session and she suddenly shouts out 'Yes, it all makes sense now. I'm going to kill myself when I get home.'

Dilemma 2: Counselling competence

Linda is a newly qualified private practitioner offering low-cost counselling. A couple ring Linda wanting couples-counselling – they say that she is the only counsellor they have found whom they can afford. Linda has no experience of counselling couples, but would like to get some. She has very few other clients. Linda believes that if she turns them down the couple will probably not get any counselling at all.

Dilemma 3: The dangerous client

Ian's client, Stuart, recently admitted that many years ago he had molested a child. In general, Stuart seems to be gaining some insight into his problems. However, he has also mentioned that he still gets occasional urges to molest children and is not absolutely certain that he can deal with these urges.

Starting point – counsellor's own ethical dilemmas

Many counsellors find themselves looking at philosophical theories of ethics for the first time, not out of theoretical interest, but because they (or their trainers or supervisors) realize that their work will inevitably lead them to face ethical dilemmas like those listed above. Counsellors look to philosophical theories about right and wrong expecting them to be decisive, practicable and acceptable.

Philosophical theories about right and wrong

> If, as I believe, nearly all ethical theories contain some elements of the truth, the best way of constructing a viable one is to pick out the true elements in each and build them into one's own theory. (Hare, 1997, p. 126)

There is no shortage of ethical theories purporting to give answers about what is right and wrong. We shall begin by looking at three of the most influential – utilitarianism, principle-based theories and virtue ethics. As we shall see, none of these theories are beyond criticism or seem to quite meet counsellors' requirements. This often leads philosophical novices to throw their hands up in despair, muttering 'Philosophical theories are all very well in theory, but in practice they are useless.' Such a response, however natural, must be resisted. A good theory is precisely what we need, because a really good theory is one which not only resists theoretical challenges but can also be applied in practice. Our approach will be inspired by Hare's advice – to look at each theory critically, extracting the elements of the truth each contains.

Utilitarianism

> Actions are right in proportion as they tend to promote happiness,
> wrong as they tend to produce the reverse of happiness.
> (Mill, 1861)

Classical utilitarianism is neatly summarized by Mill's state-ment. Utilitarianism judges actions in terms of their *consequences,* these consequences being measured in terms of *happiness* and the reverse of happiness, and the right action is the one that *maximizes* the amount of happiness (the calculation being impartial regarding rank, gender, race, etc.). Since its first formulation by Bentham[1] and subsequent development by Mill, utilitarianism has had many advocates. Utilitarianism correctly recognizes that custom and authority are not always trustwor-thy. Moreover, it is impartial, is based on human needs and wants, and is constructive, always trying to build the best outcome. Utilitarianism appears to have much going for it.

Criticisms
Unfortunately, each of the three premises upon which utilitari-anism[2] stands faces serious objections.

1. Is pleasure or happiness an adequate measure of well-being?
Utilitarianism relies on ethical hedonism, the view that happi-ness or pleasure is all that matters. Yet, as we have seen in Chapter 2, ethical hedonism is not a satisfactory theory. As the Experi-ence Machine thought experiment shows, states of mind are not all that matter to us – states of the world also matter. This flaw leads utilitarianism to allow acts which should be prohibited. Suppose John writes a diary which he intends to be secret. John's landlady finds herself in a position where she can read John's diary. She reasons that reading it will make her happy, but will not affect John at all since he will never find out (nor will she do anything to harm John as a result). As she is a utilitarian, she

reads the diary. The flaw in her thinking and in utilitarianism is that happiness is not all that matters to John. John's right to privacy also matters, but is neglected by utilitarianism.

In our three counselling dilemmas, utilitarianism could equally be said to neglect Judith's autonomy, the couple's right to informed consent and Stuart's right to confidentiality.

2. Can we really judge everything in terms of its likely consequences?

In practice, it's actually very difficult to calculate consequences. It's hard enough to calculate the consequences of a particular move in a game of chess, but life is infinitely more complex. Real-life dilemmas, so it is claimed, are too complicated to estimate consequences. What's more, even if we could calculate consequences, it is too time-consuming to do so and we might end up rigging the calculation in our favour.

The difficulty of estimating consequences applies to our three counselling dilemmas as well. How can we estimate the chances of Judith actually committing suicide, the couple benefiting from Linda's counselling, or Stuart molesting a child?

3. Is morality about maximizing anything?

Troubling as these objections are, utilitarianism's insistence on maximization is often thought to be its weakest link. Utilitarianism can seem both too demanding and yet not demanding enough. To see the first point, imagine that everything you do is supposed to maximize the amount of happiness possible in the world. Thinking of having a nice holiday? Don't do it, give the money to worthy causes instead. Fancy a nice meal out? If you were a utilitarian, you wouldn't even get as far as the restaurant, because you would give your money to the beggar you pass on the way. Utilitarians like Peter Singer would not be put off by these examples, arguing that all they show is that our normal standards of morality are too low. But in other situations utilitarianism seems to demand us to be moral villains rather than saints. Utilitarianism's maximization principle leaves it scant regard for *justice*. Suppose three hospital patients are close to death. They suffer from a defective heart, liver and kidney respectively. Imagine that a transplant operation is technically feasible for each, but sadly no organs are available. At that moment a perfectly healthy man walks into the hospital to visit a mildly ill friend. The doctors, if they are committed to utilitarianism, are supposed to kill the visitor and use his organs to save the three dying patients. Three lives have been gained at the expense of just one. But of course everyone knows that this action would be an awful thing to even contemplate; therefore utilitarianism must be wrong. It fails because it does not recognize the separateness of people, all of whom must be treated justly regardless of maximization.

Some defenders of utilitarianism, like Hare, argue that we cannot appeal to such outlandish cases. Our intuitions are framed to deal with fairly usual cases, so we cannot rely on our intuitions in these extreme cases. So consider instead the following everyday story of average folk. Imagine Shirley can visit one but not both of two sickly relatives, Samantha and Susan, in different hospitals. They both would very much like to see her and she could say similar comforting words to each. However, Samantha is a stroppy, selfish person, who can see no further than her immediate wishes, while Susan is a much more considerate type of person. Shirley, being a utilitarian, tries to work out the benefits and costs of visiting each. Stroppy Samantha would undoubtedly be much unhappier if neglected – and so would Shirley, because of the earful she would get next time she saw her! As a utilitarian, she therefore visits stroppy Samantha and so unjustly neglects sympathetic Susan. But this, it can be argued, is clearly not fair. Once again, utilitarianism has gone astray through trying to maximize happiness rather than being concerned with a fair distribution of happiness.

In counselling, it might seem that maximization is particularly inappropriate. Jan, it might be argued, is not responsible for maximizing Judith's happiness, Linda needs to give the possible negative impact of her incompetence special attention, and Ian might be thought to have a greater responsibility to his client than to the community at large.

These objections to utilitarianism are fatal to simple Benthamite utilitarianism. But utilitarianism is a surprisingly robust and flexible system, and there are various ways to try to patch it up. Most obviously, we can replace a concern for happiness with one for well-being (which we have prepared the ground for in Chapter 2) and we can calculate general rules derived from utilitarianism to apply when we have insufficient time to calculate consequences. The third objection regarding the distribution of happiness and maximization is harder to repel. For this reason, we need to consider other ethical theories as well.

Principle-based theories

> Act only according to that maxim [i.e. principle] by which you can at the same time will that it should become a universal law.
> (Kant's Categorical Imperative)

The ten commandments are perhaps the best known moral principles, and many who have not studied philosophical ethics would perhaps assume that morality always takes this form. As we have already seen, however, the *Euthyphro* question poses a fatal objection to basing ethics on authority. This means that our counselling dilemmas cannot be resolved merely by appealing to the law or codes of ethics. Ethics requires that we have to decide whether these and other authorities and the principles they produce are actually right.

Immanuel Kant, probably the most respected principle-based theorist, recognized that authority is no basis for morality. But he was also very against the idea that morality could be based on the objects of human desire, and so was a staunch opponent of utilitarianism. Kant thought that he had found a way of deriving absolute principles of morality from reason alone. Kant's basic idea is this. If you want to be rational then you must at the very least be consistent; you have to treat like cases alike. If you think it is all right for you to tell a lie yourself, you have to acknowledge that it would be equally right for me to lie in a similar situation. This is what Kant meant by a 'universal law': everyone, not just you, should do the same thing if placed in the same position. Kant thought that this would rule out all the things that were normally thought to be immoral, like lying and breaking promises. You might want to break a promise because you seem to gain from it now. But you would not agree to the universal law that *everyone* should break promises, as the whole institution of promise-keeping, which is very beneficial, would be jeopardized. Kant thought that all the conventional moral rules could be derived from one supreme rule – the Categorical Imperative, quoted above.[3]

Kant's theory contains two great insights. One is that morality does indeed demand impartiality from us; to be moral we cannot say that it's OK for me to lie, but would not be all right for you to lie, unless there is a relevant difference between us or the positions in which we find ourselves. Kant's second great insight is that we should try to base morality on reason rather than authority. But his theory contains two major flaws. The first is that rationality alone is not sufficient to derive the universal laws – we need to consider rationality *and* preferences. We can see this if we ask the reason for wanting other people to keep their promises or to refrain from killing – ultimately it's because we do not *want* a state of affairs where people lie and kill. Utilitarian considerations of the satisfaction of preferences cannot be removed from morality as easily as Kant thought.

The second problem with Kant's theory stems from his insistence that moral rules are both very general and absolute. For example, he thought that there was an absolute rule that we should never lie – even if a murderer asked us about the hiding place of his intended victim. But in practice situations arise where moral principles clash with each other, so we *cannot* follow all principles. Each of our three dilemmas involves a clash of moral principles. Jan needs to know whether to follow the rule 'Allow the client autonomy' or 'Maximize the chances of saving her life.' Linda has to decide between 'Provide help when no other may be available' and 'Practise within your own level of competence.' In the case of the dangerous client, a decision has to be made whether to continue to work therapeutically with the client or to try to maximize child safety. The most plausible response to this objection is not to insist, as Kant did, that moral principles are absolute, but to try to prioritize and refine rules. For example, the absolute rule 'Allow the client autonomy' may become 'Allow the client autonomy unless someone's life is at risk.' Moral principles are *prima facie* (literally 'at first sight') rather than absolute obligations. What we still need to find is a way of deciding the right moral principles and how to decide between them when they conflict. One promising suggestion, advocated by R. M. Hare, is to work out those rules that lead to the greatest satisfaction of preferences of all concerned. In this way Hare combines Kantianism and utilitarianism.[4] But before concluding that this is the way forward, we need to consider a third theory which argues that *both* utilitarianism and principle-based theories are incomplete.

Virtue ethics

> The good for man is activity of the soul in conformity with virtue
> ...Virtue ...is a state concerned with choice, lying in a mean rela-
> tive to us, this being determined by reason and in the way in which
> the man of practical reason would determine it.
> (Aristotle, *Nicomachean Ethics*)

Aristotle and other virtue ethicists argue that other approaches put the cart firmly before the horse. Ethics should be concerned with working out how to be a good person, not how to do the right thing. A good person will naturally do the right thing, whereas someone who has intellectual insight alone may possess neither the motivation nor the requisite skills and habits to carry out the right action. A good person, according to virtue ethicists, is one who has the right traits of character, i.e. he or she has the virtues. The classic account of virtue ethics is contained in Aristotle's *Nicomachean Ethics* – a work aimed at instructing young Athenians how to be good *and* successful citizens. Two of Aristotle's ideas are particularly important. The first and best known is his 'theory of the mean'. Aristotle recognizes that in all situations there is a pertinent virtue. Imagine Gavin is a therapist whose client, George, has a history of violence. Suddenly, after some very challenging interventions by Gavin, George starts shouting abuse at Gavin. Gavin will need the virtue of *courage* to deal with this situation well. Courage, according to Aristotle's theory of the mean, requires erring neither in the direction of being too cowardly (for example by terminating the session and refusing to see George again) nor too rash (for example by carrying on his very challenging interventions without any concern for his own safety).

Aristotle's theory of the mean tells us that for every virtue there are two opposite vices. This is surely a valuable insight – other virtues which seem to fit this model and are relevant to counsellors and their clients include self-confidence, loyalty and trust. Aristotle's theory seems to cover other virtues – like competence and justice, of which it would seem one cannot have an excess – much less well. The doctrine of the mean is sometimes wrongly interpreted as a plea for moderation. It isn't – the courageous person will act pretty immoderately if their child is being attacked. What Aristotle is really saying is that the right action depends entirely on the situation, which leads us to the second of Aristotle's significant ideas. According to Aristotle, one particular virtue is of absolutely central importance: the virtue that allows us to appreciate important features of a particular situation and have the practical wherewithal and ability to carry out means-end reasoning to do the right thing. This virtue Aristotle calls *practical wisdom*. Aristotle recognizes that doing the right thing involves not just knowing what in general is the right thing to do (which Aristotle would say comes with another virtue, *theoretical* wisdom) but also being able to apply this knowledge to particular situations. Gavin needs to understand the situation correctly and to have the ability to carry out the necessary actions in order to be truly courageous. He needs to know whether George's verbal abuse is likely to extend into violence, and he needs to know how to convert the abuse into therapeutic insight. In the counselling room, practical wisdom requires a mixture of common sense, experience and good therapeutic technique.

Though Aristotle's ideas were neglected for many years, modern theorists interested in practical questions have begun to supplement his ideas with their own. Anthony Weston, in his excellent *Practical Companion to Ethics* (1997), suggests two practical tactics to help solve ethical problems, which he calls 'Finding the best problem' and 'Integrating values'.[5] Weston argues that many dilemmas are more apparent than real and can be avoided by finding the best *problem*, i.e. the right question to be asking and the right way of looking at the problem. Brainstorming, asking other people and lateral thinking are possible ways of doing this. Preventive ethics is another way of avoiding dilemmas. We should try to stop problems occurring – in counselling, for example, by clear contracting. Weston thinks that a combination of prevention and creative thinking will greatly help reduce the number of ethical dilemmas. However, he recognizes that there will still be some real dilemmas, for example when values conflict. In Dilemma 1 above a genuine conflict exists between those who wish to be active in suicide prevention and those who wish to fully respect the client's autonomy. Weston argues that we need to consider not the question 'Who is right?' but instead 'What is each side right about?' He thinks that both sides in a dispute have usually latched on to something that really does matter – in this case the client's life and her autonomy. Our task is to avoid polarizing values. We need to find what management guru Stephen Covey calls a 'win–win' solution – one where *both* sets of values are satisfied. The standard example goes like this. Suppose I want the window open and you want it closed. We have several ways of resolving the problem, including fighting, bullying and compromising. Covey suggests instead that we can do better. We need to go deeper and ask *why* one of us wants the window open and the other shut. We need to find out what really matters. For example, I might believe that fresh air is healthy, while you might think it is too cold with the window open. As soon as we bother to ask 'What really matters?' we get beyond polarized answers and can find a win–win solution (e.g. an extra blanket and a slightly ajar window). Weston argues that this applies to ethical issues too. For example, with the suicidal client we can agree that her autonomy and life both matter – and try to find a way to respect her autonomy and her life. Rather than denying the legitimacy of the other side, we try to incorporate it into a solution. The implication is that the ability to do creative thinking is a significant virtue for counsellors facing ethical dilemmas.

How is the list of moral virtues to be decided? The first task the virtue ethicist faces is to decide what particular traits of character are to count as virtues. Aristotle's own list, including such virtues as magnificence and right ambition but excluding compassion, humility and benevolence, now seems very parochial. A plausible modern list might include:

- Assertiveness
- Benevolence
- Candour
- Charity
- Civility
- Cleanliness
- Common sense
- Compassion
- Competence
- Conscientiousness
- Co-operativeness
- Courage
- Courteousness
- Creative thinking
- Critical thinking
- Dependability
- Diligence
- Discretion
- Empathy
- Fairness
- Faith
- Fidelity
- Flexibility
- Friendliness
- Generosity
- Genuineness
- Honesty
- Hopefulness
- Humility
- Industriousness

- Justice
- Loyalty
- Magnanimity
- Moderation
- Non-maleficence
- Patience
- Perseverance
- Practical wisdom
- Pride
- Proactiveness
- Reasonableness
- Respect
- Self-confidence
- Self-control
- Self-direction
- Self-discipline
- Self-knowledge
- Self-reliance
- Sensitivity
- Spontaneity
- Tactfulness
- Tentativeness
- Theoretical wisdom
- Thoughtfulness
- Tidiness
- Tolerance
- Understanding
- Wit.

Some of the items on this list may have caused you to raise an eyebrow. Are assertiveness and proactiveness really moral virtues, as opposed to habits that are prudentially useful? Is wit important enough to merit inclusion in the list? Is faith such a good thing, or just a legacy of our Christian heritage? Are some other of these 'virtues' culture-dependent? Aristotle would no doubt have counted humility as a vice – for him the real virtue in this area is pride. How can we decide who is right? For we cannot always be both loyal and fair, and perhaps we can never be both spontaneous and thoughtful. Aristotle says that we know the answers to these questions as long as we are educated in the right way. But this just moves the question back one stage – what is the right way to be educated? This difficulty applies to our three counselling dilemmas too. Jan's virtue of compassion leads her to want to intervene, yet respect for the client motivates her the other way. Ian's benevolence suggests that he should protect the children, but fidelity motivates him to keep faith with his client. Linda's hopefulness and courage might urge her to offer her services; however, tentativeness and humility may advise otherwise.

Conclusion

The counsellor's request for a decisive, practicable and acceptable ethical theory is not completely satisfied by any of these theories. But if we put together the valid insights of each theory we can arrive at such a theory. Virtue ethics informs us that there are certain virtues – including general ones like practical wisdom, finding the best problem and 'win–win' thinking – that we need to cultivate if we are to be good moral decision-makers and agents. Rule-based theories tell us to formulate and adhere to simple rules that we will be motivated to follow. Utilitarianism gives us a means of working out which principles and virtues to cultivate and which to follow when they conflict.[6] What we need is a practicable decision procedure which counsellors can use for their own ethical decision-making and those of their clients which takes these insights into account. In the next section I will describe such a decision-procedure, 'Progress'.

Progress toward ethical decision-making

My colleagues David Arnaud and Antonia Macaro and myself have developed a decision procedure called 'Progress' which, we hope, incorporates many of the insights from the above discussion and provides a practicable, acceptable and decisive means of resolving ethical dilemmas. Progress is described more fully in Chapter 6, and even more fully at the Progress website (http://www.decision-making.co.uk). Here I will describe the five stages and their rationale. We will then see how Progress would help Linda with her dilemma about whether to undertake some couples-counselling.

The five stages of Progress

1. *Gaining a good understanding of* the facts *of a situation.*
   As Aristotle recognized, the person of practical wisdom has a good grasp of the situation in which they find themselves.

In our counselling dilemmas, Jan needs a good understanding of what really is going on – is Judith serious about suicide, or perhaps just manipulating her? Is Linda really competent to perform couples-counselling? Is Stuart really likely to molest any children? The first stage of Progress recognizes that understanding the situation is partly a matter of gaining further information, and examining one's assumptions. Progress also acknowledges that our emotions both inform and misinform us, and attempts to take account of both (Arnaud and LeBon, 2000).

2. *Gaining a good understanding of* what really matters *in the situation.*

   Utilitarians are right in thinking that the well-being of all the parties affected matters. As we have argued, we also need to take into account rights, duties and virtues. First, we creatively attempt to build up a list of everything that might matter, from various sources such as ethical theories and Codes of Practice. Next, using critical thinking, we evaluate whether these things that seem to matter actually are acceptable, relevant and important in this situation.

3. *Thinking up options creatively in the light of what the situation really is and what matters in the situation.*

   Modern advocates of creative thinking like Weston and Covey emphasize the importance of 'finding the best problem' and 'win–win thinking'. Having a good grasp of the facts of the situation and what matters in it puts us in a good position to creatively think up options which satisfy as much as possible of what matters.

The reward for carrying out the first three stages thoroughly is that the last two stages usually flow quickly and effortlessly.

4. *Evaluating options.*

   Here we just evaluate each option from Stage 3 in terms of what was found to matter at Stage 2.

5. *Carrying out the best option.*
   Here we also devise a fallback plan, in case we are prevented from carrying out the best option, and also, in cases where we are confronted by two evils, to see how we can take preventative measures to avoid having to make such decisions in the future.

Progress in counsellor decision-making – an example

Here is a worked example of Dilemma 2, putting ourselves in the position of Linda, a newly qualified private practitioner offering low-cost counselling (you might find it useful to refer to Chapter 6, p. 158, at this stage to examine each element of Progress in more detail).

Dilemma 2: Counselling competence

Linda is a newly qualified private practitioner offering low-cost counselling. A couple ring Linda wanting couples-counselling – they say that she is the only counsellor they have found whom they can afford. Linda has no experience of counselling couples, but would like to get some. She has very few other clients. Linda believes that if she turns them down the couple will probably not get any counselling at all.

1. Gaining a good understanding of the facts of a situation
a) How might Linda's emotions be informing or misinforming her? Linda says that she alternates between excitement and anxiety when thinking about her dilemma. She is excited about the prospect of getting new clients and branching out into a new area of counselling. She is, however, anxious about actually doing couples-counselling with 'real people'. She is even more anxious about what she will say if they ask her about her previous experience. Linda realizes that how she should deal with her excitement and anxiety depends on how appropriate these emotions are. Her excitement is a good reason to take on the clients only if couples-counselling is an area where she can both get

many clients and also do a good job. Linda needs a more informed view of her competence in this area and of the potential size of the market. The appropriateness of her anxiety at doing couples-counselling is harder to assess. Is this really such a new area, or is it just a new application of her existing repertoire of skills? Linda needs to find this out. Her extreme anxiety at the potential question she might be asked actually reveals that she has not one dilemma, but two. Her second dilemma is whether to be completely open about her lack of experience at the outset. Linda feels relieved that this is an option, as she does not like the thought of deceiving anyone. But she is excited about the thought of new clients.

Emotion and object	Strength	Appropriate?	Information
Excitement at getting new clients and branching out	Strong	If she can get clients in this area and can do a good job	Linda values her counselling work. However, she needs to find out more about her competence and potential client base
Anxiety at doing couples-counselling	Strong	Not if she can use her existing skills	Linda needs to find out how different couples-counselling is, and how she can supplement her existing skills if she needs to
Anxiety at being asked about previous experience	Extreme	Yes	Linda actually has a second dilemma – about how honest to be

Table 3.1

b) What assumptions has Linda been making? Linda has clearly been assuming (possibly encouraged by her excitement at new clients) that the couple will not be able to find another therapist they can afford. If she wants to make a wise decision, she really needs to question whether other counsellors might be available. Perhaps the couple will have to travel a little further – or perhaps they actually could afford more, if they prioritized the need for counselling higher.

c) What further information does Linda need? These considerations have highlighted the fact that Linda needs more information before she can make a wise decision. The two main areas of research she needs to do are into her own competence and the availability of other counsellors.

d) What actually is Linda's problem? Linda's problem began as a black and white question about whether to take the couple on or not. She was very torn because of her conflicting emotions. She now realizes that it might not be so black and white – she has options of how open she is about her lack of experience, and how she might help them by finding another therapist

2. Gaining a good understanding of what really matters in the situation

Linda needs to work out what really matters before even trying to think more about her options.

a) Linda should begin by listing the parties involved and their rights, duties, virtues and interests. The main parties involved are herself and the couple. She feels it is in her interests to have new clients and expand into a new area of counselling. She also thinks it will probably be in the couple's interests to get some counselling rather than none at all. However, she wonders whether they have a right to informed consent regarding her lack of experience (and if she has a corresponding duty to tell them). She also wonders how honest and trustful it would be to do anything but tell them the whole story.

b) What do the law and, for professional dilemmas, codes of ethics and best practice say? The law is silent on this issue, so long as she does not fraudulently misrepresent her qualifications (which she has no intention of doing). The Code of Practice that she has agreed to suggests the following four principles:

- She should not exploit clients.
- She should work within her level of competence.
- She should refer on where appropriate.
- She should consult her supervisor when appropriate.

It is also good counselling practice to be clear about the contract with clients from the beginning.

c) What do Linda's (appropriate) emotions from Stage 1 suggest about what matters? Linda's excitement does suggest that the success of her career as a counsellor matters to her. However, her anxiety reminds Linda that she must work within her level of competence and that she should not get carried away by her excitement to take on clients she should not.

d) Looking from a different perspective, that of herself and the other parties in five years' time, what else might matter? Linda imagines two contrasting scenarios. In the first, her counselling with the couple has been successful, and she has a large and profitable practice which includes couples-counselling. The other scenario is where the case has been a disaster and has drained her confidence to the extent that she has given up counselling. These two scenarios suggest that a lot is at stake. Much seems to depend on her level of competence.

e) What would Linda like done if she was in the position of the other parties involved? Linda would like to be offered the chance to make up her own mind, given the facts.

f) Linda is asked to imagine that she has the power to put an ideal solution into place. What would it be? Why would this be a good solution – what are the values that are fulfilled if it is carried out? The ideal solution would be for Linda to wave a magic wand and be competent at couples-counselling. This suggests that being a successful and competent couples-counsellor matters to Linda.

Deciding what matters most

Linda has now compiled a comprehensive list of things that seem to matter in this case. She now needs to decide whether they really do matter, and if so, how much they matter. Table 3.2 is a list of values and the weight which Linda ends up giving them (she does this by looking at the acceptability, relevance and importance of each objective).

What matters	Importance (/5)
Linda not being likely, on balance, to harm couple	5
Linda not misleading or exploiting her clients	5
Linda working within her level of competence	5
The couple getting some counselling rather than none (as long as it is competent counselling)	4
Right of clients to informed consent and autonomously making up their own mind	4
Linda referring on where appropriate – clients should get the best care possible	4
Linda getting new clients (she is competent to deal with)	3
Linda expanding range of practice within her competence	I

Table 3.2

The list differs substantially from the list of objectives Linda began with. For example, Linda began by thinking it was important for her to get new clients. She now realizes that this is not quite true – they have to be clients she is competent to deal with. The weights assigned reflect her judgement about how ethically important each objective is, always remembering that she must give her own concerns equal interest to other people's. Looking at this list, Linda acknowledges that her inclination to take the clients on probably underestimates the ethical dimension of the case.

3. Thinking up options

Linda began with only two options: taking on the clients or turning them down. She now realizes that this was rather polarized thinking. She thinks back to her ideal solution – taking on the clients and dealing with them competently – and asks herself what is preventing her from doing this. The option of getting a crash course in 'couples-counselling for qualified counsellors' strikes her as attractive. Linda next wonders if a 'win–win' solution exists which fulfils all her ethical objectives. It seems that neither of her original options actually gives the clients autonomy. The new option of telling them about her level of experience and letting them make a choice seems attractive. Another option is to help them find another low-cost counsellor or persuade them that it's worth paying the full cost for a more experienced counsellor.

4. Evaluating options

Option 1: Take on the couple without having more training or telling them of the limits of her experience.
Option 2: Turn the couple down flat.
Option 3: Try to get suitable training, and get the opinion of her trainers regarding her competence. If they think she is competent, offer her services to the clients. Tell them that she is trained but not experienced with couples and that she could try to help them get another counsellor, if they so wish.

5. Carrying out the best option

Linda now has a solution which might well fulfil everything that matters, when both original options satisfied very little. Linda will do the couples-counselling training – which her excitement informs her is probably a good idea anyway. She will also make contact with other couples-counsellors – which might even have the spin-off of getting her better known in the area. Her only

Objective	Importance	Take on	Turn down	Train and offer services telling couple about the extent of her competence
Linda not being likely, on balance, to harm couple	5	?	YES	YES
Linda not misleading or exploiting her clients	5	NO	YES	YES
Linda working within her level of competence	5	NO	YES	YES
The couple getting some counselling rather than none (as long as it is competent counselling)	4	?	NO	YES
Right of clients to informed consent and autonomously making up their own mind	4	NO	NO	YES
Linda referring on where appropriate – clients should get the best care possible	4	NO	NO	YES
Linda getting new clients (she is competent to deal with)	3	?	NO	YES
Linda expanding range of practice within her competence	1	?	NO	YES
Conclusion		REJECT	REJECT	CARRY OUT

Table 3.3

doubt is that the clients might be put off by her being honest about her degree of experience, so not having counselling when they might otherwise. However, she reminds herself that if she was in their position, she would like to know.

Discussion

Progress is suggested as a method for helping with ethical dilemmas in counselling when, like Linda, you have some time to think about the issue. Supervisors will also hopefully find the procedure of use in helping counsellors with their ethical dilemmas. The procedure's use may also extend beyond *ethical* dilemmas – there is no reason why it cannot be used to help with other tricky decisions to be made in counselling. However, there will be some situations where you have to think and act quickly, and have not got time to work your way through a decision procedure. Jan finds herself in this position when faced with a client who says she intends to commit suicide after the session (see Dilemma 1). The best preparation is for counsellors to have familiarized themselves by working through hypothetical cases in their training. The reader is now invited to use Progress to try to answer the other two dilemmas. I believe training programmes in counselling should incorporate familiarizing counsellors with how best to deal with these and other ethical dilemmas. There will still inevitably be some cases where the counsellor feels totally unprepared. In these cases I suggest that one question should be uppermost in the counsellor's mind: 'What really matters?'

Decision counselling

Many clients come to counselling for help with a specific decision, for example about their career, or relationships, or ethical issues. For others, help with one or more decisions may be part of the bigger picture of helping them find direction in life or construct a future when presenting emotional difficulties are overcome. As van Deurzen (1999) has argued, the attitude of many existing approaches to counselling, such as unconditional positive regard or neutrality or an appeal to feelings, is not particularly helpful. I believe that helping clients make good decisions is, along with helping them toward enlightened values and emotional wisdom, a major element in tapping counselling's hidden potential. Progress is, of course, not the only way that counsellors can help clients with decisions. Other approaches worth considering are those from more general philosophical counselling, and a method I call the 'Charles Darwin Method', which directly applies the methods of critical thinking to decision-making.

Using Progress in decision counselling

The decision procedure already described, Progress, can be used in collaboration with clients to help them think through their decision-making. For examples of this in action, see the Progress website (http://www.decision-making.co.uk).

Decision counselling can help with both ethical and prudential decisions. For important prudential decisions, the RSVP procedure can help with sorting out what matters to the client before embarking on Progress. The other difference is that if one wants to approach a question ethically, one does, as suggested earlier, have to take an impartial view of the situation which one is not committed to if merely interested in one's self-interest.

Philosophical counselling and decision-making about one's career

Claire, a bright young psychology undergraduate, is experiencing anxiety over an impending career decision. Attracted by the idea of helping people, she originally intended to train as a therapist with a view to private practice, but has had a lot of pressure put on her by her parents to follow her elder brother and sister into more traditional careers – management consultancy being their preferred, 'high achievement' option. Now in the last term of her degree, she is having second thoughts about becoming a therapist. 'My parents point out that I have always been a high achiever and cannot understand how I can settle for such an ill-paid, uncertain line of work as therapy. Can philosophical counselling produce arguments that will persuade them and, more importantly, me?'

Claire's dilemma is an important one: whether to follow 'the herd' in aiming for conventional goods such as money and achievement, or to try to do something more individualistic and idealistic. While traditional career counselling can help with awareness of aptitudes and opportunities, it may neglect personal values and even pre-determine the answer toward safe and conventional paths. Conversely, one's overall vision of life provides the focus for philosophical counselling. How might it help Claire make her decision? Philosophical counselling embraces numerous techniques, including conceptual analysis, critical thinking and the application of philosophical ideas. Although all of these could be employed to help Claire, the best place to start would be an exploration of her value system via what the Dutch philosophical counsellor Ad Hoogendijk calls 'utopian thinking'. The process can be generalized into three stages as follows:

1. Envisioning one's ideal life.
2. Considering one's requirements regarding a career.
3. Assessing possible careers in the light of the above.

1. Envisioning one's ideal life – the life design
Hoogendijk suggests career-counselling clients map out a 'Life Design', in which they consider their life in five- or ten-year periods between now and when they are 80. For each period they should consider where and how they want to live, what relationships they want and what activities they want to be doing, *paying no attention to practical limitations*. It's particularly important that ultimate ends, things one values for themselves, are attained. Asking oneself questions like 'What would I like written on my gravestone?' can help reveal these – as of course would other elements from the RSVP procedure described in this book. Claire says she wants to do therapy to help people, but her inability to brush off her parents' arguments about achievement, money and security are highly suggestive that she wants other things too.

2. Considering one's requirements regarding a career

When employers size you up in an interview, they are thinking about how you fit into their plans; in this exercise the tables are turned and you evaluate *them* to see how they fit into your life design. From what she says, Claire might well want to help others, and also attain achievement, security and money. Of course, in reality one will often not be able to get everything, so it would be important for Claire to list her requirements in order of importance.

3. Assessing possible careers in the light of the above

So far the process might seem to encourage the sort of idealism that gives philosophy a bad name. The whole point, though, is not to suggest that Claire can fulfil her ideal life or career, but rather to help her achieve the most she can in the real world. Information-gathering is necessary at this stage, and conventional careers counsellors and the experiences of her siblings might provide useful input. What sort of life do therapists and management consultants actually lead? Are her siblings enjoying their achievements? Is Claire similar to them? What jobs actually are available for therapists, and how much do they earn?

The use of conceptual analysis, creative thinking and critical thinking

The Life Design exercise forces Claire to think about her ideal world, her career, and the relevant facts, for the period of her whole lifetime. The exercise will be even more useful if key concepts and suppositions are made explicit and analysed. A key question to ask Claire would be this: to what extent is she persuaded by her parents' *arguments*, or is it just a case of not wanting to disappoint them? And if the latter, then is fulfilling one's parents' ambitions a good reason for a career choice? On the other hand, how reliable is a twenty-year-old's vision of her whole life? She may feel idealistic now, but will she do so in ten years' time, especially if she has a family to think about then? The life design and her counsellor's gentle but firm challenges would help her think through these issues. Conceptual analysis will also help her make a better decision. Claire and her parents are both concerned about 'achievement', but what is it? It would be useful to spend some time considering clear cases of 'achievement' and 'non-achievement' to work out when something really counts as an achievement. The procedure given in Chapter 6 on pages 144–8 would come in handy here. Claire and her counsellor might well decide that for something to count as an achievement it must also be desired and difficult to attain, as well as actually achieved. If this is what an achievement is, then would management consultancy actually be a higher achievement than therapy? There remains the question of whether therapy is a secure and well-paid profession. Some creative thinking might be of value here. Rather than setting up as a private practitioner, could she could do something like therapy *within* the business world? Perhaps she could aim to be a consultant with a special interest in helping people – for example in achieving work satisfaction. Perhaps she could even become a careers counsellor herself.

A career choice viewed as an existential choice

The decision Claire is making is of course an existential one – she is deciding what sort of life she is going to have, and what sort of person she will be. Existentialists such as Kierkegaard would say that such choices are part of the human situation. The anxiety she feels now is termed 'existential anxiety' and is the price people pay for being free. Rather than trying to rid oneself of anxiety, we should use it as a spur to think seriously about life. Is Claire going to be a conventional commuter with 2.4 children? Or does she want to achieve what the humanistic psychologist Abraham Maslow called 'self-actualization', to be all that she could be? Philosophical counselling does not automatically endorse one view or the other, but it would try to help Claire make an informed choice in the light of a critical appraisal of her values and the facts. In so doing, the aim would be that Claire, ten or twenty years from now, might avoid 'existential guilt', the feeling that one has not lived up to one's own expectations of life.

The Charles Darwin method of decision-making (CDM)

Having returned from his voyage on the *Beagle*, the 28-year-old Charles Darwin's thoughts turned to marriage. Being a rational sort of fellow, he did not want to undertake such a momentous decision as marriage without having thought very carefully about it. So he took two pieces of paper, and on one wrote the word 'Marry' and on the other 'Not Marry'. On the first sheet he listed the reasons for marrying (such as companionship) and on the other sheet the reasons for not marrying (such as being forced to visit his future wife's relatives). He decided that the reasons for 'Marry' were stronger. History records he married Emma Wedgewood within the year, that the marriage was a happy one and that it produced ten children (Burkhardt and Smith, 1986). Darwin's method can be strengthened by using the criteria of truth, relevance and strength to assess reasons for and against a decision, borrowed from critical thinking (described in Chapter 6).[7] The resulting procedure can be applied not only to decisions, but also to beliefs and judgements (and, as we shall see in Chapter 4, can also be applied to emotions).

1. State the conclusion you wish to be satisfied about (e.g. that you should get married).
2. Test the conclusion by searching for good reasons both for and against it.
3. For each reason, first ask whether it is true. If not, revise it so that it is true, if you can (for example by changing it to a statement of probability). If you do not know if it is true, you may need to note that you need more information before making a decision.
4. Ask yourself whether each reason is relevant to the conclusion. If not, ask whether it can be made relevant by adding

another premise. If it cannot be made relevant, then ignore the reason as a red herring.

5. Ask yourself how strong the reason is for or against the conclusion.

6. Go back to Stage 3 until you have assessed all the reasons in this manner.

7. Make the decision according to the relative strength of the reasons for and against the conclusion.

I would like to use an example of my own irrationality to illustrate how the process might help with decision-making by assessing the rationality of *desires* and *preferences*. For many years I had a strong desire to visit Nepal. Although I didn't reflect very much on them at the time, looking back there were a number of reasons why I wanted to go to Nepal. Probably most importantly, friends I admired had said how much they had enjoyed going there and what a great place it was. I too imagined trekking through the mountains, literally feeling on top of the world. This attraction was heightened by the idea that Nepal was home to the gurus, wise men who would give me the answer to the meaning of life. As the years went by and I failed for various reasons to make my trek to the promised land, my desire heightened into something approaching an obsession. It got to the point where I was willing to build my own – and my wife's – plans for the year around going to Nepal. Well, eventually we made it to Nepal, but the trip did not pan out quite as expected. We saw little evidence of wisdom: in fact we were fairly horrified at the superstitious and sometimes barbaric practices still being carried out, and the lack of freedom existing in society. The mountains were, it has to be said, inspiring, but after a while even they became quite monotonous. To my dismay I found myself yearning for the green fields of my native England. Add to this some unanticipated features such as ill health and (yes, I am afraid it got to me) the lack of good food and creature comforts, and my Nepal dream turned into something more like a nightmare. How might Charles Darwin have prevented my disappointment regarding Nepal? I should have made my unreflective desire to go to Nepal reflective, by examining my reasons for going to Nepal. I could then have used the 'True/Relevant/Strong' test to see if they were good reasons. My reflection might have gone something like this:

My reasons for the desire to go to Nepal:

1. My friends enjoyed going to Nepal.
2. It would be stimulating and enriching to encounter the wisdom of the people.

Reason 1, though true, turned out not to be relevant. I should have asked myself whether I was like them in relevant respects, and whether my itinerary matched theirs. Reason 2 presupposed that Nepal contained lots of wise people whom I would be able to understand and appreciate. The falseness of these positive reasons was compounded by my failure to appreciate the negative aspects of the trip, which might have been expressed by the 'Cons'.

My reasons against the desire to go to Nepal:

1. The risk of being ill, so not being able to enjoy it fully.
2. Missing the 'creature comforts' of normal life and other possible holidays.

A final feature of my irrationality was the *strength* of my desire to go to Nepal – possibly connected with the number of times circumstances had prevented me going there. In general, we can be certain that there will be plenty of causal factors which affect the strength of desires which would not survive a moment or two's reflection. We can generalize my Nepal experience by saying that in order to criticize desires, we need to, first, think about what presuppositions they depend upon, and second, try to imagine what the desire's satisfaction will actually be like for us.[8]

We can then use CDM to reflect upon whether the desire and its strength are rational.

Having presented three different methods, it remains to say something about their relative merits. The Charles Darwin Method is the most general, since looking for and evaluating reasons can be applied to beliefs, desires and emotions as well as decisions. It can also be done relatively quickly and in an *ad hoc* way – one can ask people about reasons and help them assess them as part of the cut and thrust of a normal counselling session. Progress incorporates parts of CDM, and arguably provides a more comprehensive guide, using creative thinking and theories of ethics and emotions as a resource as well as critical thinking. Philosophical counselling is more open-ended than either, so can adapt itself to the needs and style of the particular client. Perhaps once again it is a false polarization to say that we have to choose between the three methods. Decision counselling can involve using each of the methods discussed, as and when appropriate. I will conclude with some general, non-philosophical points which I think are important for the success of decision counselling.

1. Be clear that making a decision is the client's agenda as well as yours.
2. Be collaborative.
3. Be empathic.
4. Be challenging.

The ideal decision counselling session is one where the client and counsellor are together looking at the issues collaboratively. Decision counselling needs to be challenging, and so the client has to accept and welcome the philosophical spirit of the enterprise. Empathy, of course, is, as always, a necessary part of the therapeutic alliance – exploring difficult decisions relating to careers, relationships and ethical issues is hard enough as it is; for the decision counsellor being human is not an optional extra to being a good creative and critical thinker.

Conclusion

Both counsellors and their clients are frequently faced with decision-making dilemmas. The review of ethical theories showed that although they contain many insights, none fulfil the requirements of practicability, acceptability and decisiveness. Progress, an integrated method which incorporates many of the strong points from these other theories, was presented as a way of helping solve counsellors' ethical dilemmas. Progress, together with the Charles Darwin Method, also forms a core part of the toolkit of the decision counsellor, whose task it is to help clients make good decisions.

Part 2
The Emotions, Reason and the Meaning of Life

4 | The Emotions and Reason

MANY CLIENTS COME TO THERAPY hoping for release from emotional distress, such as anxiety, fear, depression, guilt or anger. Others, who come for reasons more connected with growth or being the author of their own lives, will be equally concerned with understanding and shaping their emotions. In order to try to help either type of client, it is clearly desirable for counsellors to have a good understanding of the causes, logic and meaning of the emotions. Such an understanding will clearly be informed by a number of disciplines. The study of neurology is obviously relevant to explain emotions as a biological phenomenon.[1] Psychology is also important, for example to assess the empirical support for theories of emotion.[2] Without denying the importance of neurology and psychology, it will be argued here that a *philosophical* understanding of the logic and meaning of emotions is equally crucial. Two philosophical questions about the emotions are of particular relevance to counsellors:

1. *What is an emotion?* Once we know what an emotion is – whether it is a feeling, cognition, disposition to behave or some combination of these – we will be better able to help clients make sense of their emotions and overcome negative emotions.
2. *What is the relationship between reason and the emotions?* Are they inevitable enemies locked in mortal combat, or can they be harnessed to work together?

We will begin by looking at three theories of the emotion and use the insights gained to evaluate how three of the philosophical forms of counselling – cognitive–behavioural therapy, philosophical counselling and existential–phenomenological counselling – deal with the emotions.

Three theories about the nature of emotions

Emotions are feelings

> [An emotion is] nothing but the feeling of a bodily state, and it has a purely bodily cause. (James, 1948)

Emotions often involve bodily feelings. When frightened we may experience a sinking feeling in the stomach; when anxious we may sweat; when joyful we may feel an inner glow. In general, physiological changes in our body accompany the experience of emotions. The simplest, and for many years most popular, theory about emotions is that they *are* these physiological changes and our awareness of them. As well as William James, Descartes and Hume both held versions of this view. An important implication of this view is that emotions are things that just happen to us – we have no more control over physiological changes of anger, anxiety or pride than we have over tickles, aches and pains.[3] We *fall* in love, are *overcome* with grief and are prey to our emotions. This does not, however, mean we are completely powerless to avoid emotional distress. We may be able to influence emotions by chemical intervention – for example drugs like Prozac[4] work by altering our physiological reaction to external events.

Emotions are cognitions

> Men are moved not by things but by their interpretations.
> (Epictetus)

Two people will often have different emotional responses to the same situation. It is plausible to attribute this emotional divergence to their contrasting thoughts, beliefs and judgements about the event. For example, suppose Gary and Helen are walking down the road together. Kate, a friend of theirs, walks by, but ignores them. We can easily imagine them responding to Kate's behaviour in very different ways. Gary may get very upset and feel 'down' for the rest of the day, while for Helen the incident may have no emotional consequences whatsoever. What separates Gary and Helen is not the external event, which was the same, but their *interpretations* of the event. Their response will depend both on their beliefs regarding the event and their evaluations of its importance. Gary, for example, may believe that Kate saw him but deliberately snubbed him. Furthermore, let us suppose that Gary harbours romantic designs concerning Kate. In that case Gary will regard Kate's rebuffal as a terrible thing, perhaps implying that Kate does not reciprocate his feelings. Helen, on the other hand, may believe that Kate did not see her. Perhaps Kate was day-dreaming. Anyway, thinks Helen, if Kate doesn't like me, so what? This example illustrates the Stoic philosopher Epictetus's famous dictum, quoted above. In modern parlance, it is one's beliefs and evaluations – one's cognitions – that are a central element of emotion.[5] If emotions are cognitions, then following Epictetus and the Stoics, we can try to influence emotions by altering our cognitions.

Emotions are dispositions to behave

An angry man may pound the table, slam the door, or pick a fight. The angry man is predisposed (more likely) to emit certain operands [produce desired results] rather than others. (Skinner and Holland, 1961)

Proponents of the behavioural theory of emotions would say that the acid test of emotions is behaviour. How would you find out whether your partner really loved you? Would you try to measure their sensations when they see you? No, because we do not expect someone who has been married for 30 years to feel a flutter every time their beloved walks into the room. Would you try to assess their thoughts and judgements – for example, does loving someone imply, as Plato argues, that one thinks that they are beautiful? Probably not, because we can love someone while entertaining all sorts of negative beliefs and evaluations about them. No, the acid test of love – and other emotions – is, according to this view, behaviour. Love ultimately means being disposed to behave in a certain way toward your beloved. This does not of course imply that you will be uniformly affectionate and charming to them, but it does mean that you will do what you can to help if their welfare is seriously at stake. This theory, which is associated with Ryle in philosophy, and Watson and Skinner in psychology, can be applied to other emotions too. Anger is the disposition, as Skinner and Holland suggest, to engage in activities like slamming doors and picking fights. An anxious person is disposed to flee from the situation and avoid it in the future.[6]

Discussion

We have outlined three competing theories about the nature of emotions. Clearly they cannot all be right. On the other hand, it is difficult to see how they can be completely wrong. Emotions usually do involve feelings, seem to be logically tied to beliefs and evaluations, and appear to be closely associated with dispositions to behave in certain ways. The most promising solution is that the theories err in being overstatements. While these theories claim that emotions are just one thing, in fact emotions involve all three components.

The component theory of emotion

If each theory contains part of the truth, we may hypothesize that each emotion contains a feeling, cognitions and a disposition to behave. But are these the only components, and how do they interact? To answer this let us closely examine the life-cycle of an emotion using a concrete example.

The case of Tom and the burglar

Tom, a pensioner, is sitting alone in his house, reading an article in the local paper about burglars posing as meter-readers. His mood is one of mild anxiety. Tom's doorbell goes. He hears the doorbell and realizes that there is someone at the door. The thought crosses Tom's mind that the person at the door may be a burglar and that he may be burgled. He would rather the doorbell had not rung. Tom detects a tightening in his muscles. He is in two minds about what to do: he wants to answer the door, to see who it is; on the other hand, he is inclined to sit tight in his chair to avoid the possibility of being burgled. He does nothing, and eventually relaxes a little when he hears footsteps moving away from his house. For a few hours after, though, he is a bit shaken.

A component theory which attempts to combine the feeling, cognition and behavioural accounts of emotions might characterize the episode in this way:

1. Situation prior to emotion

i) A person, with their emotions, beliefs, attitudes and desires, in their current mood. As Heidegger says, at any one time we are attuned to the world in a certain way, i.e. we are in a particular mood. We also have a set of beliefs, attitudes, motivations and desires. Tom's being a pensioner, alone, reading the article, sets the scene for his strong emotional reaction to the doorbell ringing.

ii) An event. Emotions are intentional, they are about something, and therefore require an event to trigger them.[7] If the doorbell did not ring, or Tom did not have any thoughts, his emotional tone would be unaltered.

iii) The person's perception, interpretations, beliefs and inferences about the event. As Kant realized, we do not perceive the world as it is, but through the personal 'spectacles' of our senses and our mood, beliefs and attitudes.[8] Typically we also go beyond our initial perceptions to make further inferences. Tom hears the doorbell ring and infers that this may be a burglar and that he may be burgled.

2. The emotion itself

i) Evaluation about the personal significance of the event. Emotions result only when an event is evaluated to be of personal significance. If I tell you that my next-door neighbour was on holiday last week, it is unlikely to touch you emotionally. If I say that *you* have won a free two-week holiday in the Seychelles next July, then you are likely to respond very emotionally. Tom clearly judged the doorbell ringing to be bad.

ii) Physiological change, feelings and sensations. As William James suggests, emotions usually involve a physiological change and a resulting feeling or sensation. Tom felt a tightening of his muscles.

iii) Evaluation about how to respond to the emotion and resulting desire to act. The Stoics suggested that an emotion includes a judgement about the appropriate way to react, as well as about its personal significance (Sorabji, 2000). According to the Stoics, we can choose whether to have an emotion at all and how to express the emotion. The latter evaluation about how to respond to the emotion often results in a desire to act and action itself. Tom was too paralysed by the fear to indulge in this type of thinking during the incident, though he might have reflected on it later ('It was only someone delivering the paper – how silly of me to get so worked up!').

3. Consequences of the emotion

i) Action. The desire for action at Stage 2 (iii) often actually results in action. In Tom's case inaction is the result, as Tom procrastinates and misses his visitor.

ii) A person, their current mood and their beliefs, emotions, attitudes and desires. The emotional cycle ends with the person and a – possibly different – mood, set of beliefs, attitudes, emotions and desires. Tom is now more anxious than he was to start with, and may well be even more fearful the next time the doorbell rings. On the other hand, he may dismiss it as the over-active imagination of an old man and be perfectly calm after a few hours.

Is the component theory of the emotions correct?

If correct, the component theory of the emotions has significant implications for counselling. In particular, by giving such a central role to cognitions, it challenges the view often expressed by clients that emotions are just things that happen to them over which they have no control (these clients are of course implicitly subscribing to the 'feeling' theory). The component theory opens the way for counsellors to help clients gain by reflecting on the cognitions associated with their emotions. Before we can reach this conclusion, we need to look at two challenges to the component theory, the first from neuroscience, and the second from philosophy.

Do all emotions involve conscious cognitions?

Recent brain research reported by LeDoux (1999) casts doubt on the idea that all emotions involve conscious cognitions. Even though all emotions are about something, the findings suggest that this does not imply that we always make a conscious judgement. LeDoux's study suggests that emotions do not always follow the thought/feeling sequence implied by my example. Recall that Tom perceived and interpreted the event (1iii), had a number of beliefs and evaluations (2i) and only then experienced a sensation (2ii). LeDoux argues that sensations can, in some cases, precede the cognitions, so that experiencing the sensation (2ii) will come before the belief and evaluation (2i). While his experimental findings relate only to rats and sounds associated with fear, his explanation of the nervous system makes extrapolation to human beings and other emotions plausible. Sound is signalled to the brain by one of two routes. The 'fast track' message goes to the primitive amygdala area of the brain and from there to other areas of the body. Crucially, at this stage we have only a primitive, non-verbal evaluation of good or bad. We have no conscious beliefs about what is present, or why it is good or bad. We get these only when messages go via the 'slow track' to the more sophisticated brain cortex, which takes twice as long. Usually there can be interaction between the amygdala and cortical parts of the brain. But sometimes the amygdala's reactions are too strong to overcome. These findings threaten the component theory of emotions in two ways. First, it suggests that it may have the order wrong. Cognitions may come *after* bodily effects, so cannot cause these effects. Moreover, some emotions may not even involve any cognitions at all. In ascribing reasons for these emotions, we may merely be rationalizing. We know that we are frightened, but we only guess that we were frightened by the loud noise. The emotion is a result of what LeDoux calls the cognitive (as opposed to the Freudian) unconscious.

What are we to make of this recent research? First, two caveats are in order. LeDoux's research applies only to animals. Moreover the experiments applied only to fear, and only related to sounds causing fear. There are good evolutionary reasons for fear to involve 'fast tracks' which may not be shared by other emotions, such as sadness, love, pride, shame, embarrassment, resentment and jealousy. But LeDoux's findings are congruent with common emotional experience. We are not always able to control our emotions, no matter how hard we try. This applies to love, jealousy and embarrassment, for example, almost as much as to fear. Clearly the neuroscientific research should be followed with interest. For the moment, the research justifies revising the components so as to allow the evaluation (2i) to come after the sensation (2ii) in some instances, and to allow for feedback between the two brain systems.

Are emotions meaningful?

One aspect of emotions apparently omitted (so far) from the component theory of emotions is that emotions might be meaningful. However, as Pascal said, 'The heart has its reason which reason knows not of.' There are two distinct ways in which emotions might be said to be meaningful. As has already been suggested (p. 43), emotions are not blind passions but expressions of our value system. This is actually already implicit in the component theory as stated. If emotions involve beliefs and evaluations, then we can investigate emotions to find out the underlying value system of the individual. For example, if Graham envies Jon, we can ask Graham exactly what it is about Jon that he values. So one way in which emotions are meaningful is that they express our values. Other philosophers, notably Jean-Paul Sartre and Robert Solomon, have argued that emotions are meaningful in another way – they are *purposive*. Sartre famously described emotions as 'magical transformations of the world' (Sartre, 1939). Just as the fox in Aesop's tale deemed the out-of-reach grapes to be sour, so our emotions help us to perceive the world to be more as we would like it. The contemporary American philosopher Robert Solomon broadly endorses Sartre's view. His influential work *The Passions* (Solomon, 1993) adds the idea that emotions are to be seen as primitive (and not necessarily very effective) attempts to boost our self-esteem.

The following example illustrates both Sartre's and Solomon's points. Imagine that you are in the middle of an argument. You notice that you are becoming angry. Your anger magically transforms the situation from one where *you* may be wrong into one in which *your opponent* is in the wrong, boosting your self-esteem. Were Tom to behave along neo-Sartrean lines, he might become angry at the police for doing nothing about the spate of burglaries, transforming the world from an anxiety-provoking place to one where he is judge and the police are in the dock. Tom might in general adopt strategies of fleeing from uncomfortable situations by getting angry. His anger is, in an unreflective way, motivated and purposeful. Emotional behaviour makes a sort of sense, even in cases when it is not in our long-term interest.

Should we amend the theory so that it allows for emotions to be purposive? The theories of Sartre and Solomon are not without their critics. As Jon Elster (1999) points out, it cannot be taken seriously if intended as a claim about *all* instances of *all* emotions. For example, is my joy at seeing my beloved really primarily to boost my self-esteem or change the world? However, the less bold claim that emotions are *sometimes* purposive merits serious attention. How else could one explain characters like Mr Woodhouse, father of Jane Austen's heroine Emma? Mr Woodhouse is a hypochondriac very opposed to change. Today he would doubtless be labelled a 'control freak'. What interests us about Mr Woodhouse is his habitual use of pity as a way of dealing with change. Rather than facing up to the possibility that change might be a good thing and that his change-free life is not the best possible, Mr Woodhouse chooses to pity anyone who has to alter their routine, however joyful the change may appear. A striking example is when Emma's governess, a Miss Taylor, leaves the household to make a very good and happy marriage. This change is potentially doubly distressing for Emma's father. Not only is his routine being altered, but he is also reminded that people do leave home to get married. One day, perhaps, Emma will get married. Rather than face these uncomfortable thoughts, Mr Woodhouse labels the newly-wed governess 'poor Miss Taylor'. For Mr Woodhouse, and surely for many others too, some emotions do sometimes appear to serve a purpose. A theory which ignores this aspect of emotions is not complete; we therefore need to incorporate it into the component theory. We could accommodate it by adding that the situation prior to the emotion involves a way of 'being-in-the-world' as well as the other elements. Mr Woodhouse's way of being-in-the-world inclines him to feel pity whenever anyone has to undergo a change in their routine. However, I prefer to say that what we are faced with before and after an emotional episode is a whole person – not just their cognitions.

The revised component theory: life-cycle of an emotion
The two challenges to the original component theory, from LeDoux and Solomon/Sartre, lead to the strengthening rather than the abandoning of the component theory. The revised theory can be summarized as follows.

Situation prior to emotion
1. A person.
2. An event.
3. The person's *unreflective* perception, interpretation and inferences relating to the event and later (if at all).
4. The person's *reflective* perception, interpretation and inferences relating to the event.

The emotion itself
1. A primitive feeling and desire for action via amygdala *and/or*
2. Evaluations about the personal significance of the event and the appropriate response.
3. Feelings and sensations.
4. Evaluation about how to respond to the emotion and resulting desire to act.

Consequences of the emotion
1. Action.
2. A (possibly changed) person.

For philosophically minded counsellors, these two revisions are double-edged. The meaningfulness of emotions makes unravelling emotional meaning an important task for counsellors, but the workings of the cognitive unconscious make behavioural and physiological interventions attractive. We will explore these implications later in this chapter, when comparing the various forms of emotion-focused therapies.

The emotions, rationality and emotional wisdom

There are two distinct but related questions about the relationship between rationality and the emotions. The first question is about whether reason can influence the emotions. This is a question we will look at below when evaluating cognitive–behavioural therapy (CBT). While the fact that beliefs, evaluations and desires for action are part of an emotion suggests an affirmative answer, LeDoux's theory of 'fast-track' emotions implies otherwise. The second question, which we will consider here, is at the heart of many a dispute between rationalists and romantics, which is whether we *should* be ruled by the emotions or reason – by our hearts or our heads. This question is relevant to counsellors because it affects how we evaluate CBT as opposed to existential–phenomenological counselling (EC). For philosophical counsellors, the question is of particular interest because the nature of emotional wisdom is a likely subject matter of counselling.

On the one hand, following the Stoics, we can argue that, because emotions are based on beliefs and judgements, they can be *baseless* in that they may be based on false beliefs or false judgements. This train of thought leads us down the road of Stoic therapy and cognitive therapy, in which we attempt to monitor and alter the beliefs and judgements that precede and accompany negative feelings. The Stoic philosopher Seneca, for example, emphasizes the way in which emotions such as anger can lead to experiences we do not value (such as shouting at people). He suggests that there are rational means of avoiding these disturbing emotional experiences. For example, we can reduce our disposition to anger by engaging in daily meditations. Seneca recommends specific meditations aimed at reducing our tendency to evaluate things as bad. For example, we can daily remind ourselves that life is such that things often do go wrong, for everyone. Other meditations can bring to mind the effects of our allowing ourselves to get into certain emotional states – Seneca used to tell himself how ugly he looked when angry. Conversely, 'emotions as value' theorists like Pascal and Kupperman provide an argument for taking heed of our emotions. Kupperman's suggestion is plausible because of the cognitive content of emotions. Admiring someone involves a judgement that the person we admire has some quality that we would like to emulate, while despising someone suggests the opposite. Envy implies not only the *belief* that someone possesses something, but also the *value judgement* that what they have is desirable. We are angry when we believe that someone has breached a standard that we decide should be maintained. Emotions provide information about our values.

How can this apparent contradiction be resolved? Stoics and many modern cognitive therapists, taking anger, envy and other 'negative' emotions to be undesirable, give us a technology to help us avoid them. 'Emotions as value' theorists show us how to make use of emotions, as information, even for 'negative' emotions. The discrepancy is resolved once one realizes that these two theories both need to recognize that the beliefs and judgements on which emotions are based should be well grounded. Stoic therapy errs in assuming that strong emotions such as anger and fear are *always* groundless. Their theory depends on the doctrine that virtue is the only good, and everything else (such as health, money and status) is only a 'preferred indifferent'. REBT errs in a different direction, in assuming that happiness is the only good. If one takes the more defendable view that there is a plurality of values, then it no longer follows that emotions which do not lead to happiness should be avoided *per se*. Whether they are appropriate or not depends on the individual circumstances of what the real situation is (e.g. whether someone is really in danger) and what a correct evaluation of the situation is (e.g. whether being in danger is a bad thing). As Aristotle said, 'The mild-mannered man . . . is provoked only in that way and at those matters and for that much time as the situation dictates.' So an acceptable cognitive therapy would not tell us to quell our emotions in general; but neither can the 'emotions as values' theory be maintained in an unqualified form. If emotions are partly comprised of judgements and beliefs, they can be false as well as true just like other judgements and beliefs.

Consider Ralph, who is single and is envious of his friends who are married. Should this envy tell him to try to find a wife? Not necessarily. His envy may be based on unfounded beliefs – for example the belief that married people are in general happier than single people, and that he himself will be happy if married. Second, his envy may be based on values which are dubious – for example he may think that there is a God-given duty to get married. Kupperman is right that emotions are a sense of value – but they are not a very reliable sense. Emotions are best seen as a clue to where value may lie, rather than as a final arbiter of what is really valuable.

The conclusion is that we should neither always follow nor quell our emotions. Emotional wisdom requires us to appraise our emotions, ask ourselves what reasons we can give for them, and determine whether these reasons are well founded. This process is part of the wisdom Reinhold Niebuhr suggests in the Serenity Prayer:[9]

> God grant me the serenity to accept the things
>   I cannot change;
> Courage to change the things I can;
> and Wisdom to know the difference.

Niebuhr's sentiments are endorsed by the above analysis, except that serenity, courage and wisdom are not qualities to be granted by God, but by reflecting on one's own life. What we need first is an accurate perception of reality, of how things really are. Given this, we need Senecan serenity to accept the things we cannot change, and Nietzschean courage to battle on through adversities and change the things that can (and should!) be changed.

Emotion-focused counselling

Three types of counselling – cognitive–behavioural therapy (CBT), philosophical counselling (PC) and existential–phenomenological counselling (EC) – lay claim to being both philosophical and emotion-focused. In this section I will attempt to sketch how they deal with emotions, and then to reflect on their strengths and weaknesses in the light of the above analysis. It is important to note that the objections suggested are *possible* objections, which the subsequent discussion often qualifies. Indeed, my aim is ultimately constructive and what really excites me is the possibility of synthesizing these very different approaches to help the client attain emotional wisdom.

Cognitive–behavioural therapy (CBT)

Theory of the emotions

CBT proposes an 'ABC' model of the emotions.

Activating event	This is the actual event.
Beliefs and evaluations	This is the client's beliefs and evaluations which lead to the emotional consequences.
Consequences	These are the emotional consequences.

This could be applied to the case of Gary as follows:

Activating event	Kate walked past Gary without saying hello.
Beliefs and evaluations	Gary fancies Kate.
	Gary believes that Kate saw him.
	Gary believes that Kate has snubbed him.
	Gary thinks that Kate does not fancy him.

Gary thinks that it is awful that
Kate does not fancy him.

Consequences   Gary is very upset.

Note that the beliefs include very specific beliefs about the situation (e.g. Kate saw him) as well as more general, longer-lasting and underlying beliefs and evaluations (e.g. Gary fancies Kate).

Monitoring negative emotions and the accompanying automatic thoughts

The first stage of CBT consists in teaching clients the ABC model, and in particular how to recognize the beliefs and evaluations that lead to the emotional consequences. The beliefs and evaluations are called 'negative automatic thoughts'. Clients are trained to keep a log of their emotional experiences, and to write down their associated situation, emotion, and automatic thoughts. They are also asked to rate the strength of the emotion and how much they believed the automatic thoughts on a scale of 0 to 100. This helps them monitor the improvement reaped from applying CBT. For example, Gary might write down:

Situation	*Emotion (0–100%)*	*Automatic thoughts (0–100%)*
Kate walked	Upset (80%)	Kate has snubbed me
past me	Sad (60%)	(100%)
without saying		Kate does not fancy me
hello		(95%)
		This is awful (90%)

Challenging automatic thoughts

At the same time clients are taught that many automatic thoughts which are the source of negative emotions are *irrational*. They are given a list of errors in thinking, and also ways to deal with the errors in thinking (see pp. 161–2 for a representative list of the errors in thinking). Gary would be asked to try to work out what errors in thinking applied and provide rational answers to them. He might come up with the following:

Automatic thoughts	*Error in thinking and way to correct error*	*Answer (given by Gary using CBT)*
Kate has snubbed me (100%)	This is jumping to conclusions. From the evidence, I do not know that Kate has snubbed me. There might be other explanations – such as she didn't see me.	Kate probably did not snub me – she probably did not notice us.
Kate does not fancy me (95%)	This too is jumping to conclusions, as above. Even if she snubbed me, it may be for a different reason than that she does not fancy me. She might be angry with me (perhaps for being with Helen!), or playing hard to get.	There is no good reason at all to infer that Kate does not fancy me.
This is awful (90%)	This is catastrophizing the situation. Even if Kate does not fancy me, this is part of life – sometimes I don't fancy people who fancy me! I might prefer it if everybody thought I was great, but that is not realistic.	Kate not saying hello to me isn't awful at all. I should check whether she fancies me in other ways rather than indulging in this fruitless melancholy!

Challenging underlying core beliefs and evaluations

An important element of CBT is that the beliefs are not just specific to a particular situation: there may also be very general 'core' beliefs at work. Cognitive therapists use the 'downward arrow' technique to uncover and challenge these underlying beliefs.[10] The downward arrow technique involves deliberately buying in to the initial automatic thoughts rather than challenging them. For example, rather than challenge Gary's belief that Kate does not fancy him, the therapist would say 'So, suppose she does not fancy you, why does that matter?' Gary might answer, 'It's awful for romantic feelings not to be reciprocated by the other person.' The *underlying* belief is then challenged using the same errors in thinking and ways of correcting them as with more situation-specific beliefs and evaluations. This can be summarized as follows:

Core belief	Error in thinking and way to correct error	Answer (given by Gary using CBT)
It's awful for romantic feelings not to be reciprocated by the other person (100%)	This is a clear case of Gary being upset by making an unrealistic demand on the world. Clearly not every person he finds attractive is going to reciprocate. Gary is imposing a 'should' (everyone I like should like me) and is also catastrophizing.	It would be preferable if those I fancied returned the compliment – but sometimes this does not happen. There are plenty more fish in the sea . . .

Reassessing one's automatic thoughts and emotions

Finally, Gary would be asked to reassess first how much he believed in the automatic thoughts, and also to re-rate the emotion:

Emotion (0–100%)	Revised	Automatic thoughts/Core belief (0–100%)	Revised
Upset (70%)	20%	Kate has snubbed me (100%)	30%
Sad (60%)	30%	Kate does not fancy me (95%)	5%
		It's awful for feelings not to be reciprocated (100%)	10%
		This is awful (90%)	5%

As you can see, by identifying and challenging his automatic thoughts and core beliefs associated with his being upset and sad, he is now much less upset and also less sad. The core belief of expecting reciprocation of his feelings has been challenged effectively, so he should not feel unduly upset or sad in a similar situation again. Moreover – and this is a considerable strength of CBT – Gary is now armed with a technique to use the next time he experiences *any* negative emotion. Monitoring and challenging thoughts is a skill, so Gary would be expected to become more and more proficient at the technique until it becomes second nature.

Critique

Although the example of Gary is hypothetical, it could be matched many times over by similar, real-life cases. CBT can indeed alleviate emotional distress and so is to be taken very seriously as a philosophical, emotion-focused form of counselling. Yet the analysis of the first part of this chapter suggests a number of possible criticisms of CBT, which we will now examine.

Objection 1: CBT wrongly assumes that we always have automatic thoughts and that these thoughts cause the feelings

The first tenet of CBT that can be challenged is the idea that we always have automatic thoughts (e.g. Woolfolk, 2000). Clients often claim that they cannot remember what thoughts they had before an emotion (e.g. anxiety). In these cases they may be asked to imagine a stick-figure with the emotion and put words in a bubble coming from its mouth. The anxious stick-figure might be imagined to say 'They are all going to laugh at me', the angry stick-figure 'How dare you ignore me?' However, introspection tells us these thoughts do not always precede emotions. This is backed up by LeDoux's research findings, which suggest that 'fast-track' emotions will not have thoughts preceding them. In this case, the objection can be made that all we are doing is rationalizing, making up reasons that seem to fit our emotion. Perhaps CBT has erred in trying to extend itself from relatively gradual and long-lasting phenomena, like depression, for which it was originally formulated, to emotions like anxiety and anger which are usually relatively sudden and of a short duration. While it is easy to be convinced that we have negative automatic thoughts during an episode of depression, it is less obvious that we always have any thoughts at all when anxious or fearful. Even when automatic thoughts do occur, it is questionable whether they *cause* the unwanted feeling as suggested by CBT's ABC model. If thoughts do occur during fast-track emotions, they happen *after* the feeling, so can hardly be the cause. LeDoux's research findings, together with introspection, certainly suggest that claims about causation made by CBT theorists need to be qualified.

It is an empirical question as to how damaging this objection is to CBT. As philosophers, we can imagine five different worlds, of decreasing attractiveness to the cognitive therapist.

World 1. Every emotion is preceded by conscious beliefs, inferences and evaluations. In this world it is impossible to feel anger without such thoughts as 'He has smashed into my car', 'That's all his fault!', 'He should have been more careful', 'People like him should not be allowed on the roads' crossing my mind.

World 2. Every emotion is preceded by cognitions, as above. In this world, though, we are not always conscious of these cognitions – they are automatic thoughts which go on in the background. However, we can train ourselves to become aware of these cognitions by careful monitoring of ourselves during emotional episodes and we can thereby influence our feelings.

World 3. Some emotions are not preceded by cognitions at all. During these fast-track emotions we perceive something as, for example, frightening, before the information reaches the cortex, from which all cognitions arise. However, in this world some emotions are like the emotions described in Worlds 1 and 2. Moreover, even in cases of fast-track emotions, once the information reaches the cortex we can make conscious cognitions which can radically alter the emotion.

World 4. This world is like World 3, except that the fast-track emotions are so overpowering that conscious cognitions can do little to affect the emotion.

World 5. This is the cognitivist's nightmare, where all emotions go by the fast-track, and conscious cognitions can make no difference to emotions at all.

Which world is closest to reality? Everyday experience rules out the world where every emotion is preceded by conscious cognitions (World 1) and where cognitions make no difference at all to emotions (World 5). Sometimes we do just have emotions without having any conscious thoughts (e.g. you hear a loud bang) and sometimes we can influence the course of an emotion by conscious evaluation (you realize it was just a firework). It is up to scientific research to tell us whether our world is most like the intermediate Worlds 2, 3 or 4. There may be no universal answer, of course. It may be that some emotions are more usually 'fast-track' and overpowering (World 4), others more associated with cognitions of which we can be conscious (World 2). One possibility is for more behavioural techniques to be incorporated into CBT. LeDoux suggests that the hard-wired signals to the amygdala may be eradicated by conditioning – hence phobics, for example, may not be helped so much by purely cognitive strategies because of overpowering fast-track emotions. But they may be helped by behavioural techniques such as systematic desensitization and flooding if these can change the 'hard-wiring' of the amygdalic system. An alternative is to focus more on underlying core beliefs than conscious automatic thoughts, in the hope that future 'fast-track' emotions will not get initiated, because the client will perceive the situation in a different way.

Objection 2: Cognitive therapy's catalogue of types of errors in thinking could benefit from more philosophical sophistication

On pages 161–2 we list a number of 'errors in thinking' that CBT teaches clients to detect and correct. Faulty perceptions (caused by a negative mental filter) and faulty inferences (caused by all-or-nothing thinking, over-generalization and jumping to conclusions) are both countered. So too are faulty evaluations about the personal significance of the event ('should' statements, discounting the positive, magnification and labelling) and faulty evaluations about the appropriate way to react to the event (personalization and blame). The first thing that strikes one is that this list of faults is remarkably one-sided. All of the inferential errors are cases where our thinking leads us to believe the situation is worse than it actually is. While it may be the case that depressed people tend to make negative inferences, research suggests that, if anything, most other people err in the other direction. In this case, CBT is actually making us *less* rational, in the sense that it is making us correct our inferences in only one direction, and that is the direction in which they need least correction. To go back to our example of Gary, Helen and Kate, we could argue that Helen should be open to criticism as much as Gary, because she may have erred in her inference that Kate is daydreaming.

When we come to CBT's (and, even more so, REBT's) view on 'should' statements, we reach thornier philosophical issues. To quote from one popular (and good) manual on CBT, statements like 'People should keep their promises' and 'I should have been able to do that' are 'the types of statements which create disappointment with oneself, guilt, shame, frustration and anger with others. Such excessively high standards and expectations are not compatible with our all-too-human day-to-day performance and, therefore, imply continual failure and bad feeling' (Blackburn, 1987, p. 39). Blackburn's first example is of a *moral* should – making claims about what people ought ethically to do; and her second example is of a *prudential* should

– what I ought to do in my own long-term interests. CBT's position – that we would be better off not making this sort of statement, and should talk only in terms of preferences – is very radical, if not entirely new.[11] Both claims are debatable. It is not clear that we would be better off prudentially by avoiding 'shoulds'. Certainly we would be calmer, and have less negative emotions – but is that all that matters? Would the great inventors, artists and writers have achieved all they did without being driven by some absolute 'shoulds'? The benefits of cognitive therapy (especially REBT) are closely linked with those of hedonism. It offers the client the promise of positive rather than negative states of mind. This is not a benefit to be dismissed lightly, despite the reservations we have expressed about hedonism. Anxiety and depression, for example, involve states of mind we have good reason to want removed, other things being equal. If cognitive therapy can offer us this, then it has much to recommend it. But well-being is more than long-term happiness: it's about a positive state of the world as well as a positive state of mind (see Chapter 2). If cognitive therapy results in people putting up with a less-good state of the world, it may *reduce* their well-being even if they are happier. It may, metaphorically, place them in the Experience Machine.

When we turn to the ethical 'should', the cognitive line is even more dubious. Blackburn's own example – that we would be better off not thinking that people should keep promises – is hard enough to swallow. But what about other examples? Is it merely 'preferable' that people do not murder us? Is it merely preferable that people are not cruel to children? Teaching people that there are some things that are absolutely wrong (such as murder and lying) has the beneficial effect that people do not consider doing absolutely wrong things, even when it is in their interests. If we taught children that lying or killing was only not to be preferred then, yes, the cognitive theorist is right that they would feel less guilt and other negative feelings in later life – but this would come at a high price.

The third category of evaluations that cognitive therapy

speaks of are those about how it is appropriate to react to an event. For example, even if Fred was at fault for bumping into your car, your appropriate emotional reaction may not be anger, and your appropriate behaviour may not be to thump him. CBT recommends clients do a 'cost-benefit analysis' of particular reactions, i.e. one thinks about what are the costs and benefits of acting in a certain way. Dryden, from the position of REBT, argues that some emotions are always irrational, and suggests a more 'healthy' version of the emotion. Dryden's list is as follows (Dryden, 1995, pp. 23–30):

Unhealthy	*Healthy*
Anxiety	Concern
Depression	Sadness
Anger	Annoyance
Guilt	Remorse
Shame	Regret
Hurt	Disappointment
Jealousy	Concern for one's relationship
Unhealthy envy	Healthy envy

Dryden's list is interesting, and in many ways commendable. I, personally, agree with Dryden that remorse, where one tries to atone for one's wrongdoing, is much more constructive than guilt, where one may punish oneself without any gain to anyone. I also applaud Dryden for departing from the purely hedonistic philosophy of REBT. A strict hedonist would not recommend sadness as a rational emotion at all. Nevertheless, Dryden's list, and any other list of 'rational' or 'irrational' emotions, still runs the risk of imposing the therapist's own value system on the client. Ultimately it depends on *what really matters* as to whether, for example, shame or regret is the appropriate response to, say, embezzling money from a charity. If one believes in the Aristotelian view that virtue is what matters, and being an honourable person is a virtue, then shame is a much more appropriate response than mere regret. REBT might do well to consider other, less value-laden ways to avoid negative emotions. For example, clients often feel guilty in situations where they could not have helped but do what they did. Ethical theory tells us that 'ought' implies 'can'. Guilt is not the appropriate emotion in situations where they could not have done otherwise. A second distinction that can help is Hare's distinction between two levels of moral thinking. For example, in *Sophie's Choice* (Gaarder, 1995), Sophie felt that she ought not to have allowed one of her babies to be killed. Hare would agree that, at the intuitive level, Sophie is correct – she has a *prima facie* duty to protect her baby. Yet at the critical level, where we consider what we have an *overall* duty to do, it is nonsense to say that she ought to have protected it. In her position, it was the lesser of two evils. Regret rather than guilt or remorse is a much more appropriate reaction in such cases.

Objection 3: CBT underestimates the meaningfulness of emotions

It is ironic that cognitive therapy be criticized for underestimating the meaningfulness of emotions, because this is one of the benefits often claimed for it. Beck's classic *Cognitive Therapy and the Emotional Disorders* (1991/1976) devotes a whole chapter to 'Meaning and Emotions' where he argues that it is the concern for conscious meaning that makes CBT superior to both behaviourism (which is concerned only with objective external stimuli, i.e. external events) and psychoanalysis (which labels conscious meanings as being superficial). It *is* true that cognitive therapy is extremely concerned with conscious meanings and interpretations; however, this concern has a purely instrumental purpose. Cognitive therapists are interested in meanings only so that irrational beliefs can be eradicated. I have argued at length earlier that existentialists are right in thinking that emotions can also be meaningful both in the sense of revealing the client's value system and being purposive. Cognitive therapy appears insufficiently interested in exploring the client's values (except insofar as it wishes to correct them) and to ignore the purposive nature of emotions. To this extent, CBT is likely to achieve symptom removal rather than emotional wisdom and enlightened values.

Conclusion

How effective these objections are depends on a number of things. It depends on the correctness and extent of 'fast-track' emotions – which of the five worlds do we live in? It also depends on the aim of cognitive therapy. If it aims merely to remove symptoms without regard for someone's total well-being, then perhaps it need not be so concerned with the other objections either. However, for those who see counselling as being about more than symptom removal, then a way of incorporating explorations of value (such as using RSVP) and meaning (as in existential therapy) might be attractive. Some of these ideas are brought together in Chapter 6, where more philosophically sophisticated ways of correcting the errors in thinking identified by CBT are suggested.

Philosophical counselling (PC)

Philosophical counselling, as instigated by Gerd Achenbach in 1981, is not based on the so-called 'medical model' in which mental illnesses are diagnosed and treated in a way analogous to physical illnesses. PC is much more concerned with achieving emotional wisdom than alleviating emotional distress. In philosophical counselling, theories (including the counsellor's) are not taken as necessarily correct, but form the starting point for a dialogue with the client. Suppose Paul, a single thirty-something, comes to PC confused about the nature of true love. Counselling might begin by reflecting upon various philosophical ideas, such as that attributed by Plato to Aristophanes in *The Symposium*, the classic philosophical tract about love. There the Greek comic poet recounted the myth that humans were originally happy four-legged, four-armed creatures. But Zeus thought humans too proud and so he split us into two-legged, two-armed creatures to teach us a lesson. Ever since, so the story goes, the severed halves have wandered the earth searching for their other half. Like them, according to Aristophanes, we are all looking for our perfect match. Love is a desire for two souls to become one. Aristophanes' view could usefully be contrasted with that of Antoine de St Exupéry's in *The Little Prince*.[12] St Exupéry suggests that *commitment* is the secret to true love rather than the qualities of the beloved. Far from having to wander the four corners of the earth for one's unique other half, love can work with anyone, given the right attitude.

Paul's counsellor would explore with him the possible implications of both views for his predicament. Had Paul spent too long searching for the perfect soul-mate, who would make up for all his own shortcomings? Had he unwittingly taken on board unrealistic *Four Weddings and a Funeral* expectations from our culture? On the other hand, is it really true that one can have a successful loving relationship with just *anyone?* Surely one has to find them attractive, and have some interests in common?

This leads on to the key question – what is love? The discussion in the first part of this chapter about the nature of emotions in general would of course be highly pertinent. There, it was argued that feelings, judgements and the predisposition to certain actions are all necessary conditions for emotions. It was suggested that maybe behaviour is the acid test of love. Paul might well counter this by pointing out that 'falling in love', being strongly associated with physiological reactions, may be different from the love of 30 years of marriage. The discussion could be enlightened by considering examples. Was 'true love' the lightning bolt of Romeo and Juliet or was it more like the admiration and social ties of a Jane Austen match? What about the success (or otherwise) of arranged marriages? These could all be discussed, along with Paul's own experiences. Which of his own relationships exemplified which sort of love, and which were most successful?

Paul might conclude that his original question, 'What is true love?' was the wrong question. The definition of love matters less than understanding the type of relationship that would best enhance Paul's life. How should relationships feature in Paul's life as a whole? What is the value of different sorts of relationships?

This type of dialogue would help Paul become much clearer about love and how relationships should feature in his life. PC can equally form a good basis for dialogue about other emotions of concern to clients – anger, jealousy and resentment, for example. Moreover, PC is not confined to dialogue about specific emotions. A client might be interested in exploring whether one should be swayed by one's head or one's heart, in which case the section on 'The emotions, rationality and emotional wisdom' (pp. 95–7) of this chapter could be a useful starting point of discussion. In all these ways, PC attempts to help the client toward emotional wisdom.

Critique
Objection 1: PC does not alleviate emotional distress
There's no doubt that philosophical counselling *can* alleviate emotional distress. In *Plato Not Prozac!* Lou Marinoff describes numerous case studies where philosophical counsellors have helped remove depression, reduce anxiety or control anger. One of the more interesting cases concerns a monk who had been depressed for some time, and rued how his depression prevented his faith being meaningful to him. Psychological interventions and medication had not worked, but through philosophical counselling he realized that he had, in Marinoff's apt phrase, 'been looking through the wrong end of the telescope'. It wasn't his depression causing the loss of meaning; it was the other way round. Through philosophical counselling, the monk was able to explore and re-evaluate his reasons for being a monk; he decided to leave the monastery and his depression lifted. Common sense tells us that we can be depressed when life loses meaning or value; hence reflecting on meaning in life (Chapter 5) and on the nature of the good life (Chapter 2) can help depression – at least in *some* cases. Similarly, anxiety

often results from worrying about important decisions. The methods described in Chapter 3 therefore describe constructive ways not only to help making decisions, but also of reducing the anxiety that occurs when we put off making decisions, or make them badly. Nevertheless, something about this objection sticks. Although it is untrue to say that PC does not alleviate emotional distress, it is fair to say that it *cannot promise* to do so. Clients interested *purely* in the removal of symptoms are best referred elsewhere.

Objection 2: PC requires the client to be a philosopher rather than an ordinary person

Some may consider PC to be expecting rather a lot of the client. Talk of an equal partner in dialogue may sound very laudable and democratic – but is it actually realistic to expect this of philosophically untrained clients, particularly when they are in an emotional crisis? There are several possible responses to this criticism. One is to bluntly assert that philosophy is easy and anyone can do it. But while it's certainly true that some writers make philosophy a lot harder than it needs to be, some people are not natural philosophers, just as some people are not naturally sporty or artistic. What about the people who have philosophical potential but no current expertise – how are they to pick up the philosophical methods required (conceptual analysis, critical thinking and the rest)? One possibility is for the counsellor to do most of the philosophical work, but this has the disadvantage that the client will be no better able to deal with future issues. A second alternative is for there to be an element of *teaching* in PC. This may make alarm bells sound amongst more client-centred readers, but they should remember that there are more and less heavy-handed ways of teaching philosophical methods. Three obvious but useful rules are to avoid jargon, to use examples from their own experience, and to go at a suitable pace. A final alternative, which I favour, is for the counsellor to lead the way in applying the methods (such as RSVP and Progress as well as conceptual analysis and critical thinking) but to try to get the client to increasingly do the work themselves. Once again, the objection that PC expects too much from the client is overstated, but does have some force. In my experience, really good sessions, where the dialogue takes on a life of its own that transcends specific methods or theories, are with gifted philosophers – though this is not the same as saying that the clients have academic philosophical qualifications!

Objection 3: Even if PC leads to intellectual insight, emotional insight will be elusive

Counsellors often talk about the difference between intellectual insight (where one sees something intellectually but may not really 'feel' that it is right) and emotional insight (where one feels and thinks that something is right). Intellectual insight results in clients hesitatingly agreeing – 'Yes . . . but' being a common way of expressing this. Emotional insight is indicated by clients being thoughtful for a moment or two and then saying 'Ah-ha, that's exactly it!' in an excited voice. In my view, emotional insight comes when an idea fits in with a client's own experience. For example, if Paul, the confused thirty-something, has been spending his adult years searching for his perfect match, the Aristophanes story will result in emotional insight – otherwise, merely intellectual insight. This is a strong argument for a philosophical counsellor – and other counsellors – taking a phenomenological approach, where they try to explore the meanings and experiences of the client. Good philosophical counselling is not a lecture on philosophy, nor even on practical philosophy, but a search for a meeting place of ideas and the client's own experiences.

Existential–phenomenological counselling (EC)

Theory of the emotions

Existential counsellors take their cue from the theories of emotion suggested by Sartre and Solomon as described above.

First, emotions are not to be treated as pathological, but as meaningful. Existential guilt is the call to conscience that tells us we are not living up to our standards; existential anxiety (*angst*) reminds us of our responsibility to life (as in the case vignette of Claire, pp. 73–7). These familiar ideas can be extended to seeing all emotions as revelatory of what Freddie Strasser calls a world-view. Strasser has pulled together and synthesized existential therapeutic ideas in his excellent book *Emotions* (Strasser, 1999). Strasser argues that emotions always have a meaning, they reveal someone's worldview. In particular they reveal their values, sedimentations (a concept he takes from Spinelli) and ways of maintaining their self-esteem. Emotions can be experienced in unreflective or reflective mode, and one of the main purposes of therapy is to allow the unreflective to become reflective. Reflecting on emotions allows our worldview – our values and sedimentations – to emerge, enabling the client to explore and challenge parts of it.

Strasser illustrates how these ideas work in practice in his case study of Amelia, who defines her problem as an uncontrollable anger. Therapy involved exploring this anger in detail – when it happened, how it felt, its costs and benefits. A turning-point occurred when Strasser explored her anger with *him* over a small incident in therapy. Amelia felt anger but was reluctant to criticize him for fear of losing his approval. This confirmed a recurring pattern of an 'ugly Jewish girl' attempting to preserve her self-esteem by the twin strategies of gaining approval and trying to be perfect. Extreme anger resulted both from emotion not being expressed for fear of rejection and as a way of preventing her feeling inferior.

Whereas Amelia's anger was previously unreflective, she was now aware of her strategies and could start to challenge them. Strasser empathized with her predicament and encouraged her to challenge both her sedimented belief that she had to be perfect and her negative assessment of herself. As therapy proceeded, his interventions became less frequent, and the client in effect became her own therapist. Writing after the conclusion of therapy, Amelia confirmed that although she still got angry, her anger was no longer uncontrollable; her awareness of its patterns and sources no longer led to her holding damaging grudges. It is important to note that EC not only helped her change, it also helped her make sense of her emotion. If emotions are a type of language, they are not a language we readily understand. Existential–phenomenological counselling offers a (student-centred) tutorial in comprehending the language of one's emotions.

Critique

This case reveals both the considerable strengths, and some potential criticisms, of the existential approach. Some of its strengths, in terms of exploring the meaning of emotions, have already been emphasized. Another considerable strength is that its emphasis on unreflective emotions and sedimented beliefs offers a palatable alternative to those – like the present writer – who do not buy into the whole Freudian notion of the unconscious (see especially Spinelli, 1996). As for objections, the criticism that it cannot *promise* relief from emotional distress can be levelled at EC as much as PC. I will now consider some specific objections to EC.

Objection 1: Existential–phenomenological counselling (and existentialism) overstates our ability to just 'choose' our emotional responses

It is a caricature of existentialism to suggest that it thinks people are completely free. To be sure, existentialists think that we should not treat habit, custom or the practices of our society as an excuse for not deciding for ourselves, but this is a far cry from the view that we are free to do as we please. In some places, though, Sartre does write in ways to support the caricature. One such place is where he reclassifies emotions as 'actions' rather than 'passions'. We are, according to Sartre, as responsible for our emotions as we are for our actions. The component model of emotion endorsed above casts doubt on Sartre's view. In particular, we should think carefully before assigning responsibility for 'fast-track' emotions. But if we cannot choose our fast-track emotions, can we at least choose which situations we put ourselves in? For example, a violent man can choose to keep a safe distance between himself and a firearm. Moreover, as CBT suggests, we can influence our cognitions and hence our 'slow-track' emotions. The unique contribution of EC is the notion that by reflecting on our way of being-in-the-world in counselling we can change it, if we so choose, which will affect our future emotional responses – as Amelia chose not to react angrily so often. If emotions are not to be reclassified as actions, as Sartre thinks, they are certainly far from being passions. Clients are encouraged to open themselves to exploring their emotional reactions at their own pace, and in making the unreflective reflective can indeed become more the author of their own lives.

Objection 2: Emotions are neither reliable indicators of value nor universally purposeful

A second objection, which gets to the heart of existentialist assumptions about the emotions, is to cast doubt on both strands of the idea that emotions are meaningful. We have already argued that although, as Kupperman suggests, emotions are analogous to a sense of value, they are not a reliable sense. Hence existential therapists should avoid treating emotions as if they are proof of value. As was argued in Chapter 2, emotions should be used as indicators of 'candidate values' which then should be assessed on their merits – a way of doing this is provided in the RSVP procedure (see pp. 149–57). Probably more significant in existential practice, though, is the idea that emotions are purposeful. Amelia's anger prevented her from feeling inferior, and I recognized a similar phenomenon in some situations in my own existential therapy. Although the idea that *all* emotions are always purposeful is rather far-fetched, as long as existential therapists tentatively open up the possibility for the client that emotional responses may be unreflective strategies, then this may not matter so much.

Toward an integrated philosophical therapy of the emotions?

It is very easy to criticize each of these theories; less easy to try to construct a viable integrated therapy of the emotions from the acceptable parts of each – but this is something that should be attempted. Before discussing how this might work in practice, I would like to briefly discuss one attempt that has already been made to develop a more philosophical version of cognitive therapy by the American philosopher and counsellor Elliot Cohen. His ideas are neatly summed up by the title of his book – *Caution: Faulty Thinking Can Be Harmful to Your Happiness* (1992). Cohen gives the example of a man who became anxious whenever buying a car. Questioning by Cohen revealed that the man held the view that 'All car dealers are slime-balls' which, naturally enough, led to anxiety whenever confronted by a car dealer. Once this belief was challenged as being an over-generalization, the man's anxiety when buying a car subsided (Cohen, 1995). The trick is not only for the counsellor to point out faulty inferences in sessions, but also for the client to become aware of the thoughts behind his emotions *as they happen* and to analyse them and correct them himself. What is being advocated by Cohen is a more philosophically sophisticated ('logic-based') form of CBT. This could take two forms. One would be where, as Cohen suggests, one teaches clients to avoid fallacies likely to affect their thinking. Cohen's point is that there are a lot more fallacies than those given in the CBT handbook – for example, see Warburton (1996). This could be complemented and made more effective by using the ideas from the Counsellor's Philosophical Toolbox to teach clients how to reason soundly (CDM, pp. 148–9), as well as teaching them how not to reason unsoundly (pp. 162–4). For all beliefs, preferences and evaluations involved in the emotion the counsellor can ask the client to give reasons, and then assess whether there are true, relevant and strong grounds for the belief, preference or evaluation.

Here is an illustration of philosophical cognitive therapy in action. Neil comes to a session in a state of anxiety. When asked why, he says that it is because he thinks he will lose his job. The counsellor then examines his belief that he will be made redundant using the Charles Darwin Method. Neil is asked to state reasons for and against believing that he will lose his job. His main reasons for thinking that he will lose his job are, first, that some people in the firm will lose their jobs; and, second, that he does not get on very well with his boss. The counsellor next asks whether these reasons are true, relevant and strong. It turns out that the belief that some people will lose their jobs is not certain – it's just a rumour, which Neil estimates has only a 25 per cent chance of being true. It is true that his boss does not like him, but when pressed about the relevance of this fact, Neil admits that his boss is probably too professional to let this influence him. Neil concludes that his belief that he will lose his job is not well founded, and he leaves the session in a much less anxious state.

Of course, philosophical cognitive therapy will not only use more sophisticated ideas about critical thinking: it will also be sensitive to the criticisms of traditional cognitive therapy mentioned above. Neil would not be told to seek happiness or avoid 'shoulds'; rather, a more subtle exploration of his value system and belief system would take place, possibly involving RSVP. However, philosophical CBT is not without its pitfalls. One of the great strengths of CBT is that it has catchy names for techniques (such as 'avoid black and white thinking') which people might actually remember at the time of the emotion and soon after. Will they be able to apply critical thinking at times of such stress? What might help (conventional) CBT is an empirical study of which fallacies actually are most common, so that they could be incorporated into the CBT framework.[13]

But it is not only philosophy and cognitive therapy that have useful insights. I would suggest that each therapy has a number of useful insights and methods, as follows.

Cognitive therapy

1. Recognizing that cognitions (beliefs, evaluations and inferences) are part of emotions.
2. Devising methods for becoming aware of and challenging:
   (a) Inferences regarding an event (e.g. Kate snubbed Gary).
   (b) Evaluations about an event (e.g. It's awful that Kate snubbed Gary).
   (c) Evaluation about how to respond to an event/emotion (e.g. Gary is upset).
   (d) Core beliefs which lead to negative emotions (e.g. people must reciprocate my feelings for them).

Philosophical counselling

1. Understanding the nature of specific emotions as applied to client (e.g. love).
2. Tackling questions about emotions as applied to client (e.g. 'head v. heart').

Existential–phenomenological counselling

1. The need for a phenomenological approach (not least to ensure emotional insight is reached).
2. Investigating the meaning (purpose and values) of emotions.

It might be argued that these three therapies are incompatible paradigms, each with their own advantages and defects, and leave it at that. Certainly they come from very different philosophical traditions. Furthermore they have contrasting therapeutic objectives – CBT of symptom removal, EC of enhancing self-knowledge and authenticity, PC of wisdom. Only a fool would try to integrate them.

Having trained in each approach, however, it seems to me that their strengths perfectly complement each other, particularly with reference to the emotions. People often come to therapy wanting alleviation from emotional distress and with little awareness of the role that cognitions play. CBT offers the former by teaching the latter. But clients also have a unique set of values and a need to understand as well as change their emotions, which EC offers. This need for a general understanding of their emotions, and of emotions and reason in general, can be further enhanced by PC. Let's briefly examine how an integrated therapy of the emotions might work by looking at the case of Brian, mentioned right at the start of Chapter 1.

Brian is sad and sometimes gets depressed, but most of all wonders how he has come to lose touch with all that he used to think important.
Brian's case is interesting, not least because it straddles the cases where someone simply wants the removal of emotional distress (as with Neil above) and where they seek emotional wisdom (like Paul). Brian's counsellor might be tempted to explore both avenues. Brian's depression could clearly be seen as a message telling him that he has deserted his values. In search of emotional wisdom, Brian would be asked about the things he used to think important. This would not be as simplistic as asking him what he thinks is important and working out how he could now attain these things. It may be that the things he thought were important are no longer important, or perhaps they never were. RSVP, or parts of it, would be an invaluable guide during this process. On the other hand, Brian's counsellor could try to reduce his emotional distress by enquiring about his depression. What happened when he felt sad? What were his thoughts preceding, during and after bouts of depression? Was Brian making faulty inferences, or were irrational core beliefs and evaluations causing the problem? Brian would be asked to keep a log of these episodes, and be taught to identify faulty thinking and its remedy.

It should be clear by now that I do not think that a counsellor needs to choose between achieving symptom removal *or* emotional wisdom – he or she can try for both. This could be achieved by exploring Brian's value system while teaching him about cognitive mistakes. Indeed, sometimes combining the two is not only desirable but also necessary. If Brian is very depressed, working with values may not be very productive as it may seem to him *now* as if nothing matters. Some initial cognitive therapy will help get him into a position where he can see things in a less jaundiced way. Conversely, in some cases talking about values early on in counselling may provide the necessary motivation to overcome his depression. If Brian is only a little depressed, doing RSVP work with him may give him a vision of what a bright future will be like and an incentive to carry on the therapeutic work. In this way the wise therapist practises the virtues of creative, 'win–win' thinking themselves – they can help the client achieve emotional wisdom and alleviate distress by taking insights from a number of useful therapies.

Conclusion

The time has passed when theorists can plausibly claim that emotions are reducible to being just feelings, cognitions or dispositions to behave. The only acceptable view – the 'component' view – is that emotions are composed of each of these. The fact that cognitions are a component of emotions has enormous implications. If emotions involve beliefs about what has happened, evaluations about their personal significance, and evaluations about the appropriate way to react, then emotions can be influenced by dialogue about these beliefs and evaluations. However, this theory can be challenged by philosophical and scientific critiques. We need to allow for the meaningfulness and purposive nature of emotions. We also need to allow that sometimes emotions come before cognitions, which means that we may need to work on changing people's worldviews – the content as well as the style. To reverse the controversial utterance of a recent British prime minister, 'We need to understand more and condemn less.' CBT provides a technology for altering emotions, EC can help clients make sense of their emotions, PC provides an open-ended forum for a more general understanding of the emotions. An ideal philosophical therapy of the emotions would combine the virtues of each approach and lead to emotional wisdom *and* the alleviation of emotional distress.

5 | The Meaning of Life

The meaning of life is the most urgent of questions. (Albert Camus)

Ours is a society that has perfected its means yet neglected its meaning. (Albert Einstein)

Philosophy and the meaning of life

For many clients, including those who are depressed, suicidal or addicted, lack of meaning in life is a serious issue. Helping the client find more meaning in life is also an attractive proposition for those practitioners who see counselling more as a journey toward growth or enlightenment than a means of symptom removal. As Einstein reminds us, our society is much better at providing means toward our getting things than helping us think about why these things really matter. Counselling has the potential to be a place where people can think through these issues. Although some philosophers dismiss the question of the meaning of life as meaningless or ignore it altogether, I believe that the question about the meaning of life is an important one and one which philosophy can help answer. We will consider two sorts of responses – those focusing on God (the theistic answer) and those that do not (the non-theistic alternative). We will then consider the implications of these views for counselling.

Is life meaningless without God?

One of the most articulate statements of the theistic answer to the meaning of life comes in Leo Tolstoy's autobiographical fragment *My Confession* (1905). At the very height of his literary success, Tolstoy found himself 'overcome by minutes at first of perplexity and then of an arrest of life . . . These arrests of life found their expression in ever the same questions: "Why, well, and then?" No answer, be it in term of his business, family or vocation could survive one simple yet devastating question – "Why?"'

> All right, you will be more famous than Gogol, Pushkin, Shakespeare, Molière, and all the writers in the world – what of it?

Tolstoy's problem was not that he was unsuccessful or unhappy. His problem was that his success and happiness were no longer meaningful to him. And even if Tolstoy could somehow catch sight of meaning, he felt that the inevitability of death would destroy it.

> All my affairs, no matter what they might be, would sooner or later be forgotten, and I myself should not exist. So why should I worry about these things? How could a man fail to see that and live – that was surprising!

Tolstoy turned to science and philosophy for the answer, but to no avail. His feelings of meaninglessness gnawed relentlessly on his sense of happiness and success; eventually he found himself contemplating suicide. Tolstoy was saved by making the leap of faith to God, the only alternative, he concluded, to unendurable meaninglessness.

> No matter how I may put the question, 'How must I live?' the answer is 'According to God's law.' 'What real result will there be for my life?' – 'Eternal torment or eternal bliss.' 'What is the

meaning which is not destroyed by death?' – 'The union with infinite God, paradise.'

In short, Tolstoy concluded, 'Without faith one cannot live.'

As one would expect, Tolstoy's *My Confession* is a beautifully written and, to many, persuasive argument for the theistic position regarding the meaning of life. We must now examine whether its substance matches its style. Tolstoy has two arguments to suggest that life is meaningless if God does not exist.

Death destroys meaning

Tolstoy's argument can be reconstructed as follows:

Premise 1: At present I care about lots of things – my writing, my family, my estate.
Premise 2: However, one day I will be dead, and my affairs will be forgotten.
Conclusion: Therefore I should not worry about these things, and life is meaningless.

We need to ask exactly why Tolstoy's mortality and the impermanence of his achievements are a good reason for him to stop caring. On the face of it, Tolstoy seems to be confusing value and permanence. Why should something have to be permanent to be of value? Is a child being tortured not a bad thing, just because it does not last for ever, and will be forgotten at some distant time in the future? Indeed, Tolstoy's argument contains the seeds of its own rebuttal. If his death is a bad thing (which he clearly thinks it is) then this must be because the things he is doing now are of value. If nothing really matters, then death is of no significance. As we have seen when discussing the case vignette of Alex (pp. 10–14), the prospect of death can actually have the reverse effect to that which Tolstoy experienced. As Popper has argued, 'There are those who think that life is valueless because it comes to an end. They fail to see that the opposite argument might also be proposed: that if there were no end to life, life would have no value; that it is, in part, the ever-present danger of losing it which helps to bring home to us the value of life' (Popper, 1977, p. 148). The most that can be conceded to Tolstoy is that death and the impermanence of our achievements decreases the total significance of our lives. This, however, is all the more reason to live every moment to the full (*carpe diem!* (seize the day!), as Robin Williams advises his students in *The Dead Poets' Society*); not to suggest that life is completely meaningless.

Why? Why? Why?

Tolstoy's second reason for thinking that, without faith, life is meaningless, is the unanswerability of the 'Why?' question. Why should Tolstoy be concerned about his estate, his writing or his children? The answer is quite simply that he should care because these are things that are of value. As we have seen in Chapter 2, there are some things that matter, and some things that do not. Those things that matter do so because they are desirable states of mind or desirable states of the world. The opposite view, nihilism, is not a serious philosophical position. Nihilism implies that nothing whatsoever matters. Some writers who are sometimes taken to be nihilists – such as Nietzsche – cared very much about some things, but were disputing the conventional values of their age. A consistent nihilist would have to be very much like the character of Meursault in Camus' *L'étranger* – someone without emotion and motivation, who is totally indifferent to their own fate. But people in general do have emotions and do feel strongly motivated about their lives. Anyone still tempted by nihilism as a general theory of value and as an argument for suicide (as Tolstoy was) should consider the following argument. Either nihilism is true or it is not. If it is true, then nothing matters, so suicide is not a particularly rational option – it's no better or worse than carrying on living. If nihilism is not true, then clearly it cannot be a good argument for suicide either. So neither way is suicide recommended. If Tolstoy replies that suicide is the only authentic way to respond to meaninglessness, then he would of course no longer be a nihilist, but someone who recognizes authenticity as a value.[1]

The Myth of Sisyphus

Before moving on to a positive answer to the meaning of life, we need to examine an influential argument which concludes that life is absurd, regardless of whether God exists. This view is often connected with existentialism and in particular with Albert Camus' *Myth of Sisyphus* (Camus, 1942). Sisyphus was condemned by the angry gods to push a rock up a mountain, only for it to fall to the bottom and the process to repeat, without end, for eternity. Camus reminds us of the endless repetition of human life.

> Rising, streetcar, four hours in the office or the factory, meal, streetcar, four hours of work, meal, sleep, and Monday Tuesday Wednesday Thursday Friday and Saturday according to the same rhythm.

Our lives, so the argument goes, are really like Sisyphus' – absurd and meaningless. Camus' metaphor is superb, and it has two very important implications – neither of which is that life is necessarily meaningless or absurd. We should begin by asking whether Sisyphus' life is meaningless. The distinction we made (on p. 29) between states of mind and states of the world is helpful here. Might meaning be found in Sisyphus' positive state of mind? Camus himself agrees that it might: 'The struggle itself towards the height is enough to fill a man's heart. One must imagine Sisyphus happy.' Sisyphus' attitude is the key. But surely Sisyphus' life has no meaning in terms of state of the world? Certainly he does not achieve anything material. The rock always ends up at the bottom of the mountain. But his attitude of scorn and defiance may inspire others – like Frankl's attitude in Auschwitz. So the first lesson that Sisyphus teaches us is that meaning can be found in the most hopeless of predicaments, one's attitude being the key to meaning, a lesson that logotherapists and Stoics would endorse. Nevertheless it must be admitted that Sisyphus' plight is not an enviable one. If human beings really are like Sisyphus, our potential for meaning may not be zero, but it is certainly limited. But how like Sisyphus are we? At this point we must remember that Camus was not only a noted philosopher but also a Nobel Prize-winning writer. His description of human life above is a masterpiece of deliberately colourless prose, omitting any of the elements that make life meaningful, such as emotion, progress and interaction with friends and family. Compare the following:

> Rise, make breakfast for children, take them to school. Start reading a new book on the way to work. Make progress towards finishing my current project. Have lunch with one of my best friends. Go home and relax with family.

Human life suddenly no longer seems quite so meaningless. So the second lesson is that Sisyphus reminds us of the qualities of bad lives. There are at least two ways of leading a bad life – not attaining one's goals or pursuing goals that do not ultimately matter. Sisyphus of course fulfils both criteria. Casaubon in *Middlemarch* is another example of a character leading such a bad life. Not only does he not succeed in completing his masterpiece, *The Key to All Mythologies*, it turns out that someone has beaten him to it, rendering the work useless and his inattention to his wife Dorothea all the more inexcusable. In the postscript to this book, I compare bad, meaningless lives to those of racing greyhounds, who not only never catch the hare, but also do not realize that it is not a real hare. My point is that while greyhounds are doomed to this fate, human beings are not.

The most sophisticated reworking of Camus' point has been made by American philosopher Thomas Nagel. Nagel, in his celebrated essay *The Absurd*, points to the discrepancy between the seriousness with which we take ourselves and the tiny significance of humanity (and each of us) from the perspective of the universe as a whole. Nagel has a point. We *do* take ourselves very seriously, yet from the point of view of, say, the star Sirius, we are like ants. But Nagel is not saying that our lives are valueless. On the contrary, he is only saying that an objective viewpoint exists which does not give our lives the significance that they have subjectively. Nagel advocates taking an ironic stance to the universe; reflecting that if nothing matters much from the viewpoint of Sirius, that fact doesn't matter either. I think that for the counsellor, Nagel's argument has two positive uses: first, to suggest to those who are finding too much (negative) meaning in their lives that there is a perspective from which it does not matter, second, it can prompt us to try to increase the amount of objective significance in our life, as Singer urges below.

What is the meaning of life?

Clarifying the question
Meaning as **purpose** *versus meaning as* **significance**

Meaning normally has two distinct, if related usages. Sometimes it means 'purpose', at other times 'significance'. If you ask 'What was the meaning of building the pyramids?' you are asking about the purpose and intentions behind their construction. If your clinical supervisor asks you about the meaning of a client being late for a session, he or she is probably asking you about its significance. Meaning as purpose refers specifically to someone's conscious intentions (the builders of the pyramids may have intended to please the gods); meaning as significance can take a much broader perspective (the significance of the lateness could be that the counselling is not going very well). Questions about the meaning of life seem to be about both – we are interested in both the purpose and significance of life. But it is quite possible that there could be purpose in a life but no significance, or vice versa, so it is important we do not get the two confused.

Meaning of the universe, humanity or individuals

But this is only the beginning of the ambiguity. We have to ask whether we are talking about the meaning of the universe, humanity, or an individual life. Actually a question about the meaning of life could be one of six separate questions:

1. What is the purpose of the universe?
2. What is the purpose of the human race?
3. What is the purpose of an individual life?
4. What is the significance of the universe?
5. What is the significance of the human race?
6. What is the significance of an individual life?

These are six very different questions. Questions 1 and 2 about the purpose of the universe and the human race as a whole seem to defy a final answer – someone of a scientific outlook might reply 'We do not know, but there is a reasonable chance it has no overall purpose – it is just the product of blind chance.' Question 3, about the purpose of an individual life, seems different. I'd want to say both that there need not be just *one* purpose – there could be many purposes, and also that this is something that we would have to ask the individual. Questions 4 and 5 about the significance of the universe and the human race again are unknowable, whereas Question 6 about the significance of an individual life seems to depend on what that individual does, and what standard you judge him or her by. Clearly we would normally say that some lives (e.g. those of Hitler and Mandela) are very significant whereas others are not. This brings out two different senses of significance – what we could term 'subjective' and 'objective' significance. 'What is the significance of her life, from her point of view?' might get a very different answer from 'What is the real significance of her life?' Someone can think their life is very significant – but it need not be. This can be because either their standards are misplaced (they think getting into the *Guinness Book of Records* is significant, but it isn't), or because they think they have reached those standards when they haven't (e.g. they think they will remain famous, but they are soon forgotten). Conversely, someone can think their life is insignificant but it could actually be very significant – again either because their standards are wrong (they think that the only significant thing is being a success in business, when it is not), or their evaluation is wrong (they actually are a success in business).

The distinction between the meaning of human life in general and of individual lives is sometimes expressed as the difference between 'the meaning of life' and finding 'meaning in life' or 'meanings of life'. Even if there is no answer to the questions about *the* meaning of life (in senses 1, 2, 4 or 5) there can still be meanings in life (senses 3 and 6). One can have individual purposes, without the universe having a purpose. One can have significance, even if we do not know the significance of the whole universe. This prepares the way for an answer. Non-theists answer that questions about the meaning of life are unanswerable and possibly not very important. But questions about meaning *in* life, or meaning*s* of life are both answerable and important.

The answer
The work we have done in this book puts us in an excellent position to provide a positive answer to the question of the meanings of life. All of the three other topics we have considered pertain to meaning.

Meanings of life and the emotions
The American existentialist philosopher Robert Solomon has suggested that emotions provide the significance in our lives. Solomon concurs with Heidegger's assertion that emotions or moods are our way of 'being tuned in to the world' and adds that they are also how we are 'turned on by the world'; a being without emotion would have a life where there was no meaning: 'Our emotions constitute our world' (Solomon, 1993). Emotions then provide much of the colour to our lives, they give it its

personal significance. Is meaning, then, just the sum of our emotions? Not quite, for meaning implies a structure as well as individual episodes. We could have very many disparate emotional experiences, but when we are asked from another perspective what it added up to, answer in the negative (which might impinge on our future emotional episodes). Emotions are a necessary but not a sufficient condition for subjective meaning in life.

Meanings of life and the ethics of right and wrong

The Australian ethicist Peter Singer has suggested how living ethically can help increase the meanings of one's life:

> If we are looking for a purpose broader than our own interests, something which allows us to see our lives as possessing significance beyond the narrow confines of our own conscious states, one obvious solution is to take up the ethical point of view, i.e. to take the viewpoint of an impartial spectator. (Singer, 1979)

We can see this in relation to our distinction between states of mind and states of the world. If we say that our well-being consists in part in positive states of mind, then our lives have a certain significance in that they carry *some* value. Such is the life of the people in the Experience Machine. However, it is easy to see that the significance of their lives is limited if one looks at the state of the world. The difference between someone who thinks they have discovered the cure for cancer and someone who actually has discovered it is one of external meaning. The significance of our lives is obviously expanded if we enhance not only our states of mind, but other people's states of mind and the state of the world. For Singer, this provides a reason to be moral. Be moral to have a meaningful existence. Being ethical is a way of increasing both subjective but, particularly, objective significance and purpose in life.

Meanings of life and well-being

There are several ways in which lives can fail to be meaningful. One way is if we do not have goals or purposes. In this case our life will not have purpose, and is unlikely to be significant, except by accident. A second way is for us to have goals and purposes, but for them to be in some way faulty. The goal does not have the properties we think it possesses. As mentioned, this is the fate of Casaubon in *Middlemarch*, who does not realize that someone else has already discovered the Key to all Mythologies. If goals and purposes are faulty, then we may have subjective if not objective meaning. We may find meaning in our lives, even if an onlooker possessing a more informed view would not categorize our lives as meaningful.[2] If we have goals and purposes which are not based on false foundations, then we have a more secure foundation for meaning in the sense of purpose. But we are by no means guaranteed significance, for our goals may be thwarted. Should I decide to try to be a great sportsman, my life might be very purposive, but due to lack of ability will be utterly insignificant, as I would be doomed to failure. Of course, once I got an inkling of this, I would most likely lose my sense of purpose too.

This analysis suggests a close link between meaningful lives and well-being. Someone who has a set of values of the type which comes from applying RSVP, and who is fulfilling those values, will lead a meaningful life in all senses, i.e. it will be both purposive and significant from both a subjective and objective perspective. It will be purposive because these values provide purpose to one's life. It provides significance because these values, by definition, are precisely those things that matter – and they matter not only subjectively (because they are your values) but objectively (because they can be defended by reason). Is well-being and meaning the same thing? No, for two reasons. First of all, as we have seen, meaning encompasses purpose as well as significance. Second, a significant life is not necessarily a valuable life. Something can be significant yet be of negative value. The life of Hitler would seem to be an example. So even if something is meaningful, we should not conclude it is of value: we should first ask whether the significance is positive or negative.

In short, meaning is connected intimately with well-being, right and wrong and the emotions. Meaning comes from getting these other aspects of life right. Having enlightened values, making good decisions and having emotional wisdom is the best recipe for a meaningful life.

Counselling and the meaning of life

About a third of my cases are not suffering from any clinically definable neurosis but from the senselessness and aimlessness of their lives. (Jung)

Jung's vague impressions have recently been supplemented by considerable research into the connection between meaninglessness and psychopathology. There is evidence to link meaninglessness with depression (Klinger, 1977) and substance abuse (Newcomb and Harlow, 1986). Yet there is a history of commentators suggesting that, however important the philosophical question of the meaning of life is, it is somehow unedifying, and we are best casting our gaze from it. Freud went as far as to say that 'the moment one inquires about the sense or value of life one is sick' – implying that only those suffering from other symptoms, such as an excess of libido, will bother with the meaning of life. Yalom, in his excellent treatment of the topic, concludes that 'there is something inherently noxious in the process of stepping back too far from life' (Yalom, 1980, p. 478) and 'the more we rationally seek it [meaning], the less we find it'. Yalom thinks that 'engagement is the therapeutic answer to meaninglessness' (*ibid.*, p. 482). 'Pure meaninglessness, especially when it emanates from assuming a detached, galactic, perspective, is best approached obliquely through engagement which vitiates the galactic perspective . . . the effective therapist must help patients look *away* from the question' (*ibid.*, p. 483).Yalom's view results from his belief that meaninglessness is part of the human condition, so we are better off not facing it. He thinks we are 'a being who searches for meaning and certainty in a universe that has neither' (1989, p. 12). Not only is this somewhat uncomfortably like 'bad faith', it also confuses the six questions about the meaning of life identified above (p. 130).

The analysis of the first part of this chapter suggests a different view. Yalom is right that meaning is best approached obliquely. But whereas Yalom recommends engagement, I advise also focusing on values, right and wrong and the emotions.The problem with engagement is that it can be either good or bad, depending on what one is engaging in. One could find engagement in helping famine, spotting trains or being a mass-murderer. Some types of engagement are more desirable than others. Engagement will lead to a subjectively meaningful life, but not necessarily either an objectively meaningful life or a good life.

How can counselling enhance meaning in life?

The argument of the first part of this chapter suggests that the philosophical approaches to counselling will enhance meaning without specifically focusing on meaning. Counselling which aims to remove emotional distress will enhance the positive personal significance of life and help increase purpose. Counselling which helps people behave in a more ethical way enhances the positive objective significance in life. Most of all, value-focused counselling will help create a framework which if fulfilled will lead to meaning. If value is not foregrounded, it means we may act from custom or habit rather than our true values – we will be inauthentic. If values are not reflected upon, it may mean that they might not stand up to scrutiny. Tolstoy's *The Death of Ivan Ilyich* is a tragic – and all too realistic – example of a man living in bad faith about what really matters in life until it is too late; my claim is that we would in general do better to think more about what really matters to us. There is one exception to this, namely that philosophical confusion can on occasions lead to meaninglessness. We will end with an example of how an eminent philosopher once helped remedy this.

Philosophical counselling and the meaning of life

R. M. Hare (in Klemke, 1981) describes the case of a cheerful, enthusiastic, sociable and non-smoking Swiss student who was staying at his house in the 1960s. One night, uncharacteristically, the student went to his room, asked for cigarettes, and went for a long walk around some damp fields, returning to be unusually silent at meal time. Questioning eventually revealed that he had just finished reading Camus' *L'étranger* and had become convinced of the truth of the utterance of Meursault when the priest tries to get him to receive absolution – 'Nothing matters', said Meursault.

Hare is not a philosophical counsellor – but he thought that as a moral philosopher he ought to have something to say to the student that would be relevant. In my view, what he did can undoubtedly be classified as one of the earliest recorded examples of philosophical counselling in the modern world. Like Socrates – arguably the first philosophical counsellor of all – Hare began the discussion by asking about the meaning of words: in this case 'matters' and 'important'. Hare and the Swiss student agreed that the words 'matters' and 'important' are used to express concern. So when someone says 'Nothing matters', we need to ask whose concern is being expressed. There are three people involved, one fictional and the other two real: the writer, the reader and the character in the novel. Is Camus' lack of concern being expressed. No, argues Hare, anyone who has produced such a good novel must care very much – he is extremely concerned about his work, and his readers.

So is it the character in the novel who is not concerned? Hare says that it's not so surprising this character is unconcerned – that is the sort of person he is. There are such people who care very little about anything, though they are very rare. (And, though Hare fails to do so, we could well connect this with Heidegger's notion that Dasein's basic state is *Sorge* – care or 'taking care'. Dasein is ahead of itself ; looking to the future; already in the world; with a certain mood; and alongside entities within the world; engaged in something (Inwood, 1997, pp. 51–2).)

Biologically and ontologically we are beings who care: 'Why', argued Hare, 'because an imaginary Algerian prisoner expresses unconcern for the world which he was shortly to leave, should my friend, a young Swiss student with the world before him come to share the same sentiments?' He *did* care a lot about many things: 'his problem was not to find something to be concerned about . . . but to reduce to some sort of order those things that were matters of concern to him; to decide . . . what he really wanted'.

The mistake of the Swiss student was to think that 'mattering was something that things did, rather like chattering; as if the sentence "My wife matters to me" were similar in logical function to the sentence "My wife chatters to me".' Hare thinks that 'Matters isn't intended to describe something that things do, but to express our concern about what they do; so of course we can't observe things mattering; but this doesn't mean they don't matter.'

6 | The Counsellor's Philosophical Toolbox

ONE OF THE MAIN CONCLUSIONS of this book is that philosophy can help counsellors not so much by providing pre-packaged answers to the traditional questions of philosophy, but by suggesting methods that can be used collaboratively with clients. In this chapter I describe five of the most important contents of the counsellor's philosophical toolbox. The first two – critical thinking and conceptual analysis – can be thought of as basic philosophical methods of use to analyse philosophical arguments and clients' issues alike. The next three – the Charles Darwin Method, RSVP and Progress – arise out of an analysis of philosophical theories, and are aimed at helping clients be more rational, have more enlightened values, and make better decisions respectively. The last section, on the philosophical methods of CBT, aims to describe some of the existing techniques of CBT and supplement them with some of the ideas contained in this book.

Critical thinking

Critical thinking is perhaps the single most useful philosophical method for the counsellor. Its value is that it enables clients to be more rational and reasonable in their decision-making, beliefs, values and emotions. Here I will sketch some of the elements of critical thinking that are most relevant to counsellors. Readers new to the subject are referred to the Recommended Reading section for more complete treatments.

A little logic

Critical thinking helps us to be more rational and reasonable in life by helping us to assess arguments. An argument consists of a conclusion, supported by one or more premises. A premise is simply a reason which forms part of an argument. Here is a very simple (and valid) argument for the conclusion that 'All philosophers are fallible.'

Premise 1:	All human beings are fallible.
Premise 2:	All philosophers are human beings.
Conclusion:	All philosophers are fallible.

The conclusion that 'All philosophers are fallible' is justified, because the reasons 'All human beings are fallible' and 'All philosophers are human beings' are both true and, taken together, imply the conclusion. This argument is an example of a good[1] *deductive* argument. A deductive argument is one where the premises logically entail the conclusion. If the premises are true, then the conclusion must be true. The critical thinking literature distinguishes several different types of argument[2] – deduction being just one of them. In fact in real life – and counselling – by far the most important form of argument is not deduction but the 'Pros and Cons'[3] type of argument. In 'Pros and Cons' arguments we look at reasons for and against a conclusion, and make a judgement about which reasons are stronger.

An example of a 'Pros and Cons' argument
Should Sandra agree to Brian's request for a date tonight?

Reason for:	Sandra has nothing else to do tonight.
Reason for:	Sandra is a bit hard up and could do with a free meal.
Reason against:	Sandra didn't enjoy Brian's company much on a previous date and doesn't think she'll enjoy his company tonight either.
Reason against:	Sandra doesn't really fancy Brian.

With 'Pros and Cons' arguments, unlike deductive arguments, the conclusion does not follow with certainty from the reasons. The premises do not logically entail the conclusion. Sandra needs to *judge* whether the reasons for going on the date outweigh the reasons against doing so. As we shall see, the fact that no conclusion follows automatically by no means implies that we cannot make a rational – or irrational – decision.

Two other forms of argument which can be important in real-life decision-making are *inductive arguments* and *arguments by analogy*.

Inductive arguments

An inductive argument is one where we infer from something happening in the past that it is likely to happen in the future. Inductive arguments rely on the known and unknown cases being similar in relevant respects, and on the past examples not happening through sheer chance.

An example of an inductive argument:

Premise: *Sunny Jim* beat *Slowcoach* on the previous three occasions they met.

Conclusion: *Sunny Jim* will probably beat *Slowcoach* when they meet today.

This argument relies on shared features between the previous occasions, such as race conditions being alike and *Sunny Jim* and *Slowcoach* being in similar form now to then. The argument would fail were *Sunny Jim* now lame, or if they were now running over a steeplechase whereas previously they had run over hurdles. Underlying inductive arguments is the assumption that some causal powers which were effective before (e.g. *Sunny Jim*'s speed and stamina) are still effective. Therefore we have to be convinced that past occurrences were not a matter of pure chance – something we can become more sure of if there is a large sample of past cases. Contrast the argument 'This coin came down heads twice so it will come down heads again' to

'This coin came down heads 99 times so it will come down heads again.'

If we notice people (including clients) making inductive arguments, there are two questions we need to ask ourselves:

1. What are the differences between the past cases and the future cases?
2. Is the sample of past cases sufficiently large?

Arguments by analogy

An argument by analogy is one where we argue that because two cases are in general similar and one case has a particular feature in which we are interested, we can infer that the other case also has this feature. While inductive arguments use many past examples to infer information about a future example, arguments by analogy argue from just one specific past case. Arguments by analogy therefore rely on there not being anything different about the second case which would cast doubt on it sharing the feature in which we are interested.

An example of an argument by analogy:

Premise 1:   A business should not overspend its budget.
Premise 2:   A government is like a business.
Conclusion: A government should not overspend its budget.

If we agree with Premise 1, then whether the argument is a good one turns on whether a government is like a business in the relevant respects. We need to know whether there are relevant differences between governments and businesses. For example, if it is easier for governments to get loans at lower rates of interest than businesses, then the argument would be weakened.

Very often people (including clients) make arguments by analogies implicitly in the metaphors and similes they use. For example, a client may say 'My marriage is like a prison.' Such imagery can have a very powerful negative emotional effect, and we need to help clients think about whether such analogies are justified. The key question is always 'Are there any relevant differences between the two cases?'

Critical thinking applies to decision-making, which means it also applies to actions, beliefs, judgements and, potentially, emotions

The example given of Sandra and the date concerns decision-making, which might seem to be a bit restrictive. But the scope of decision-making – and critical thinking – is very wide indeed. Not only do we decide about what to do, we also decide what to believe, we decide what to judge as being in our own interests, and we decide what is morally right. Many philosophers have also argued that to a large extent we also decide what to feel. If we can find a practical method for helping people to act, believe, judge and feel rationally, we will be performing a valuable service – in ordinary life, and in counselling.

Good reasons are reasons which are true, relevant and strong

For us to perform the service of helping people make rational decisions, we need to help them distinguish good reasons from bad reasons, which means we need to know what makes a reason a good reason. Fortunately, the critical thinking literature[4] provides a convincing answer to this crucial question. A reason is a good one when it satisfies three conditions[5] – namely that it is *true*, *relevant* and *strong*.[6]

Criterion 1: Truth

For a reason to be a good reason, at the very least it has to be *true*. If I give as a reason for buying a new car the fact that the new car will be more reliable than my old car, for this to be a *good* reason it must actually be true that the new car will be more reliable. Sometimes, of course, we are not in a position to know for certain whether a claim such as this is true or not. For example, I do not know whether it will be sunny tomorrow. In such cases, though, we should aim to say whether it is *probably* true based on the best evidence available. If the weather centre says there is an 80 per cent chance it will be sunny tomorrow, I would be justified in giving the reason 'The weather centre says there is an 80 per cent chance of sun tomorrow' for going on a picnic tomorrow. I would not, however, be justified in giving as a reason 'It will be sunny tomorrow' because this is not something I know to be true. Moreover, the less the probability of the correctness of a statement, the less strong the reason (Criterion 3).[7]

Criterion 2: Relevance

A good reason not only has to be true, it must also be relevant. An argument that is true but irrelevant is a 'red herring' and should be discarded. Politicians are particularly adept at throwing red herrings into arguments. When asked if their party is reducing the rate of inflation as promised in their manifesto, a politician may say that the other party did even worse when in office – a point which, however true, is beside the point. To decide whether a reason is relevant, we need to ask 'Does this reason support *this* conclusion?' The politician's answer that the other party did worse is completely irrelevant to the question of whether *they* have reduced the rate of inflation, and should be classified as a red herring and discarded.

Sometimes reasons are not relevant on their own, but become so if combined with other statements. For example, is the statement 'Businesses should not overspend' relevant to the conclusion 'Governments should not overspend?' Not immediately, but it may be if we add the premise 'Governments are just like businesses.' Similarly, the statement 'All human beings are fallible' is relevant to the conclusion 'All counsellors are fallible' only if the premise 'All counsellors are human beings' is made explicit.[8]

Criterion 3: Strength

Once we have established that a reason is true and relevant, we need to ask how *strong* it is. For example, suppose Jim is deciding whether or not to buy a new car. He cites as a reason for buying the car the fact that it will have a better CD player. Let us assume that this is true. It is also relevant, because the quality of the music system is on Jim's wish-list for a car. Is it a strong reason, though? Almost certainly not. Assessing the strength of a reason is largely a matter of judgement about how much this reason really matters.

These ideas about how to construct and recognize good arguments can be supplemented by learning about different types of logical fallacies. Weston (1992) says that there are 'two great fallacies'. The first is drawing conclusions from too little evidence, for example because the sample of cases is too small in an inductive argument. The second is overlooking alternatives, for example in thinking of possible interpretations of people's actions (recall our case of Gary being snubbed). For a comprehensive list of fallacies, see Warburton (1996).

Conceptual analysis[9]

Conceptual analysis is a way of becoming clearer about what we mean. It involves a careful investigation of language and usage including searching for definitions and drawing distinctions. In philosophical counselling, concepts central to both the problem itself and the client's worldview are subject to analysis. One of its aims is the Wittgensteinian goal of untying the knots in our thinking. The point is that our personal meanings often depend on our understanding of words; if we misunderstand a word, or are confused into thinking it has properties it has not got, this can have a very real effect – as with Hare's Swiss student described on p. 136. Far from simply 'playing with words', conceptual analysis can be a very important step. It's a vital part of the counsellor's armoury whenever a term is being used which seems central to what the client is talking about, but actually is ambiguous or vague. Examples we have come across in this book include 'autonomy', 'achievement' and 'meaning of life'. Here I describe a simple three-stage procedure which can help you and your clients do conceptual analysis.

Step 1: Look at a range of examples of usage

Think up two or more clear sentences where the term is being used positively and negatively. For example, if you are trying to understand the term 'achievement' (as Claire was in the case vignette on pages 73–7) then think up two sentences of something being an achievement, and two sentences mentioning something that is not an achievement. Also think up two borderline cases: cases which are neither clear positive nor negative cases, but which mention the term under discussion. This is what I came up with for 'achievement':

a) Positive cases
    1. It was an achievement for mankind to reach the moon.
    2. My friend Steve becoming a Professor by the time he is 40 is some achievement.
b) Negative cases
    1. It was no achievement to be the only one who could not complete the ten-mile walk.
    2. It is no achievement to breathe.
c) Borderline cases
    1. Although Liz thought she achieved a lot at school, later she realized that with her advantages it was no real achievement.
    2. Fred thought he had achieved very little; in fact his book became a best-seller.

Step 2: Attempt a definition

Now use these cases to attempt a definition of the concept. Start by trying to work out what it is about the positive cases that makes them clear examples. The type of definition to aim at is the sort that Socrates aimed at – one that tells you how to distinguish the positive cases from the negative cases. Ideally, the definition should give you *necessary* and *sufficient conditions*. A necessary condition is a prerequisite, a condition that must be fulfilled before it can count as a positive example of something. For example, it is a necessary condition of being a bachelor that you must be unmarried. A sufficient condition is a condition which, if fulfilled, guarantees that it will count as a positive example. While being unmarried is not a sufficient condition for being a bachelor (you might be female), being an unmarried male is sufficient. At this stage you should also notice different senses of the concept (as in the discussion of autonomy on p. 37) and concepts which are closely related to each other but not identical (as with 'meaning of life' and 'meaning in life' on p. 131).

For achievement, my list of necessary conditions is as follows.

Definition of achievement
Achievement is:

- Getting or doing something which is desired.
- Overcoming a situation where difficulties exist.
- Where other people, or yourself at other times, might have failed.

These three conditions are each necessary conditions (e.g. it would not be an achievement if there were not difficulties) and are *jointly* sufficient – any case which satisfies all three criteria is an achievement.

Different senses of the concept
There is a difference between a *sense* of achievement and an *actual* achievement. We get a sense of achievement when we *think* we have satisfied the criteria – an actual achievement is when we actually have done it. Pointing out this distinction will

be a great help to clients who have no sense of achievement, but have actually achieved something.

Step 3: Check that your definition is correct

Having come up with a definition, we need to check that it is correct. A good start is to check that it counts in the positive cases we came up with in Step 1, and counts out the negative cases, and perhaps helps us decide the borderline cases, or explains why they are still borderline. If we find that our definition cannot do any of these things, we need to go back to Step 2 and revise it so that it does better.

Our definition of achievement copes well with the positive cases. Reaching the moon and becoming a professor were certainly difficult, might have resulted in failure, and were desired outcomes. How about the negative cases? Breathing is not difficult, so is not an achievement, and coming last in the race was not desired – so again our definition passes the test. Let us now examine the borderline cases.

1. *Although Liz thought she achieved a lot at school, later she realized that with her advantages it was no real achievement.*
   We can now say that Liz had a *sense* of achievement, but now realizes that it was not an *actual* achievement – because although she achieved a desired outcome, it was not sufficiently difficult.
2. *Fred thought he had achieved very little; in fact his book became a best-seller.*
   Here the boot is on the other foot – Fred had no sense of achievement, as he did not think he was going to achieve anything; in fact his book was a best-seller, i.e. an actual achievement.

Having carried out the three stages of conceptual analysis, we are clearer about how to use the term under discussion correctly. As we saw with the Claire case vignette, words can have real power over us, and conceptual analysis is a good way of redressing the balance.

The Charles Darwin Method

The Charles Darwin Method is based on the method the creator of evolutionary theory used when deciding whether to get married, as described on page 77. In fact, the procedure has a very wide application, allowing us to decide whether each of the following can be justified by good reasons.

* Actions and decisions.
* Judgements and evaluations.
* Preferences and desires.
* Beliefs.
* Emotions.

The procedure for each is the same:

1. State the conclusion (action, desire, belief, emotion, etc.) you wish to be satisfied about (e.g. that you should get married).
2. Test the conclusion by searching for good reasons both for and against it.
3. For each reason, first ask whether it is true. If not, revise it so that it is true, if you can (for example, by changing it to a statement in terms of probability). If you do not know if it is true, you may need to note that you need more information before making a decision.
4. Ask yourself whether each reason is *relevant* to the conclusion. If not, ask whether it can be made relevant by adding a missing premise. If it cannot be made relevant, then ignore the reason as a red herring.
5. Ask yourself how *strong* the reason is for or against the conclusion.
6. Go back to Stage 3 until you have assessed all reasons in this manner.

7. Make the decision according to the relative strength of the reasons for and against the conclusion.

There are several examples of the Charles Darwin Method in action in this book. The example of my holiday in Nepal (pp. 78–9) shows how it can be applied to desires and preferences. The example of Neil (p. 118) shows how it can be applied to the emotions and beliefs.

The Charles Darwin Method is a powerful and versatile tool for the wise therapist, who will recognize that its very power means that it requires careful use in counselling. In particular the counsellor should be:

1. collaborative;
2. empathic;
3. challenging;
4. clear that the examination of the emotion, judgement or belief is the client's agenda as well as yours.

Developing enlightened values using RSVP[10]

RSVP is a procedure aimed at developing enlightened values. It synthesizes many of the ideas about well-being, values and meaning from the philosophical therapies discussed in this book, and from philosophical ideas about well-being. It is presented below in the style of a self-help exercise to give to clients; obviously this is not the only way it need be used. Counsellors are encouraged to use RSVP on their own values first; for its own sake, and to inform their use of it with clients.

The aim of RSVP is to allow you to think about your values, and produce a list of values which can be defended as those that would make your life go well if they were fulfilled. A value is simply something that is generally worth going for and the fulfilment of which would make your life go well. RSVP has the following five stages:

1. Thinking up 'candidate' values.
2. Grouping values together.
3. Assessing whether each 'candidate' value should be accepted.
4. Clarifying the relative importance of each value.
5. Thinking up virtues and goals associated with each value.

1. Think up 'candidate' values

The aim of this part of the exercise is similar to brainstorming – it's trying to avoid missing out things that appear valuable to you. Note that it's choosing things that *appear* valuable. Later (Stage 3) we will assess whether they really are valuable.

i) Your present values

Start by writing down a list of your ultimate values off the top of your head. For example, you might write down 'pleasure, accomplishment, autonomy, helping others, money'. Start by writing down as many good things as you can, then restrict yourself to the top five. Don't spend too long on this: there will be plenty of opportunity to add more values later. Part of the benefit of listing your values now is to measure the progress you make. For example:

1. Pleasure.
2. Accomplishment.
3. Autonomy.
4. Helping others.
5. Money.

ii) Develop more enlightened values by examining your past

The Life Review exercise

Take a fresh sheet of A4. Draw a graph marking the x-axis 'Year' (it should start with the year you were born) and the y-axis 'Well-being'. By 'well-being' is meant a subjective rating from 0 to 100 indicating how well you would say your life has been going at each point. Think for a few minutes about significant periods and events in your life, and how well your life has been going as you have got older. Now fill the graph in, annotating it with your significant life periods, events and ratings. For times that have gone particularly well or badly, try to identify what values of yours were being affected, positively or negatively. Extrapolate from this those values which seem to have been most important in affecting how well or badly your life has been going.

Alternatively, use a table with the following structure:

Age	Period	Well-being	Good things	Bad things	Values
5–9	School	70%	Lots of friends		Friend-ship
10	Last year at junior school	20%		Bullied	Popularity?

When thinking of good things and bad things, bear in mind that these can include the following sources of value:

- Achievements (e.g. getting your first job).
- Experiences (e.g. having a nice vacation).
- Habits of mind/virtues (e.g. becoming more proactive).

A useful map to check that you have included all areas of life is as follows:

- Personal (e.g. emotional life, intimate relationships, close friends).
- Social (e.g. jobs and colleagues, status).
- Physical (e.g. health, geographical location).
- Ideal (e.g. values, religion, virtues, goals).

For any of the negative events that you listed, is it possible to see any meaning in them, or some good that came out of them?

Would it have been possible to adopt an attitude that would have made them less bad? If so, add this attitude to your list of values.

What advice would you give yourself about how to live, if you could revisit the 'you' of five, ten and twenty years ago? What values do you think are implied by this advice?

The 'It's a Wonderful Life' thought experiment
Imagine that you had never lived. What difference would it have made? Do not dismiss this question with 'Not much, alas', but try to think of how, in your personal, social and professional life, you have:

1. encountered and affected other people;
2. accomplished tasks that were worthwhile;
3. experienced things that made life worth living.

Use these insights to:

1. reassess your past life (as the James Stewart character did in the film);
2. think about what values you might want to satisfy in the future.

iii) Develop more enlightened values by thinking about your future

a) What advice do you think a good friend would give you about how to live?
b) What advice do you imagine you might give yourself about how to live now – at the end of this year, at the end of the decade, at the end of your life?
c) If you had six months left to live, how would you spend it?
d) If you had to give one good reason why you should be allowed to continue to live, what reason would you give?
e) What would you like written on your gravestone (other than 'still alive')?

For each answer, ask yourself what it tells you about your ultimate values.

iv) Develop more enlightened values by looking at states of mind and states of the world

The Experience Machine

An inventor offers to plug you in to a machine which will give you the authentic experience of anything you like.

a) Design a day for yourself plugged in to the Experience Machine. What experiential values does this suggest?
b) You are offered the choice to stay plugged in to the machine for the rest of your life. Would you accept? If not, why not? What (non-experiential) values does this suggest?

Three wishes

You are given three wishes which can change the world in any way you like. What would your three wishes be? What values does this suggest?

v) Use emotions as your 'sixth sense' which detects value

Start by writing down a list of people (dead or alive, real or fictional, famous or obscure) you admire, respect or envy, and people you despise, lack respect for or pity. For both sets of people, ask what reasons you have for your attitude. Extract from this a list of values. For example, you might have written down that you admired Nelson Mandela, because he has helped other people and has complete integrity. Next, think of things that you are passionate about and those that make you angry, and ask yourself what it is about them that elicits this emotion and so what the corresponding value is.

Person/Thing	Emotion (e.g. admiration, respect, envy, despising, lack of respect, pity)	Value
Nelson Mandela	Admiration	Helping others, integrity

2. Try to group values together, and weed out things that are valued purely as means to other values

You may now have quite a long list of 'candidate values'. There are two ways to make this list more manageable:

1. Group values together where you can. For example, if three values are 'Spending time with friends', 'Being liked by friends' and 'Comradeship' then you can group these three values together under 'Friendship'.

2. Check that each value is not valued purely as a means to something else. You can do this by asking yourself about the reasons why you want it. Next, ask whether you would still want to satisfy your value if you already had what it gives you. If the answer is 'No' then it is valued only as a means, so should be eliminated and replaced by the more ultimate value. For example, suppose you have written down 'Money' as one of your values:

   a) What reason do I have for wanting money? Answer – more status, bigger house and more security.

   b) If I had more status, a bigger house, more security, would I still want money? If you answer 'No' then you should replace 'Money' as a value with the other items.

3. Assess whether each 'candidate' value should be accepted

The questions you have answered have been designed to come up with enlightened values, so there is a good chance that these 'candidate' values should be accepted. However, we need to verify that this is the case. For example, suppose your (hopefully) more enlightened list of values is:

- Positive emotions.
- Absence of negative emotions.
- Accomplishment.

- Friendships and intimate relationships.
- Intellectual stimulation.
- Helping others.

1. Imagine that all of these values are being satisfied in your life. What would your life be like? Remember to think in terms of states of the world and states of mind and each of the areas and sources of value described above. Would anything be missing? Would any of the values interfere with each other? Have you any evidence for these views (for example from the life review)?
2. Ask yourself why you think each of these things is a good thing. Again, do this in terms of states of mind and states of the world. For example, you might say that intellectual stimulation is a good thing both because it is a preferred state of mind and because it can lead to worthwhile states of the world. Next, ask yourself if you are making any presuppositions – for example, that worthwhile things can only be produced by the intellect – and whether these presuppositions can be justified.

Use your answers to identify any missing values, and also to justify whether each value should stay on your list. Do this by giving reasons for and against the value, and asking whether the reasons are true, relevant and strong (see pp. 142–3).

It is important to do this in the spirit of genuine enquiry, trying to find arguments against things even if they seem obviously good. Imagine that you are trying to convince a Martian – assume nothing. Be prepared to make your values even more enlightened by refining them slightly. For example, a reason against valuing the positive emotions is that positive emotions are not always appropriate, e.g. when a loved one has suffered a misfortune. So you might change 'Have positive emotions' to 'Have appropriate positive emotions'. If at any stage you become unclear about what a value really means, try to become clear by attempting a definition, and if still unclear attempt conceptual analysis as described on pages 144–8. Cross off any values that you are not able to defend.

4. Try to clarify the relative importance and structure of values

Ask the following questions:

a) Do some values appear more important than others? Answer this by comparing values, two at a time, asking 'Would I choose a life adopting ultimate value A or B?'

b) Do your values depend on each other in any way (do some values tend to be in conflict or are they mutually reinforcing?)?

c) Do any values exhibit diminishing returns (e.g. you might need a certain number of close friends, but beyond that you don't need any more)?

d) Which of the values are purely personal (i.e. apply just to you) and which are more universal in that they apply to most people? Is it human nature, the human condition or your own personal nature that makes this a value? For example, you might argue that friendship is a fairly universal value because humans are social creatures, but intellectual curiosity is more personal because it's just your nature to be intellectually curious.

5. Write down associated virtues and goals

You now have a set of enlightened values – all you need to do now is make sure that your life satisfies them! To help you do this, you might like to think of virtues which will help you be the sort of person who fulfils the values, and goals which will help you focus on satisfying the values and monitor whether you are doing so. A *virtue* is a habit which generally leads to the fulfilment of particular values (e.g. loyalty helps friendships). Kekes (1992) thinks that there are also a number of general virtues we need if we are to lead worthwhile lives, including self-knowledge, self-control, self-direction and wisdom. He says 'We need self-knowledge to develop a realistic view of ourselves . . . We need wisdom to understand our limitations and possibilities and to conduct ourselves accordingly. We need self-control to change ourselves from what we are to what our ideals prescribe we ought to be.'

Virtue	Associated value (if any)
_____	_____
_____	_____
_____	_____
_____	_____

A *goal* is a specific, concrete aim which brings about the fulfilment of a goal (e.g. a goal associated with friendship might be to see one's close friends at least once a month). Fill in the table below. Write a list of goals for the next year, five years and lifetime. For each goal, ask yourself your underlying reason for wanting to achieve this goal. For example, you might write down 'I want to be retired by the time I'm 50.' The associated values might include not having to work, being able to spend more time with my family and having fewer worries.

Period	Goal(s)	Value(s)
This year	Have a nice holiday	Time with family, pleasure, lack of stress
Next five years	Have work that I find financially rewarding and meaningful	Meaning, money
Lifetime	. . .	. . .

Progress:[11] A procedure for good decision-making

Progress is an integrated method for helping people make good decisions. It is intended to help counsellors resolve ethical dilemmas that arise in their work, and for use by decision counsellors to help clients make good (ethical and prudential) decisions. As with RSVP, it is given in the form of a self-help exercise, but is intended mainly for collaborative work between counsellor and client (or supervisor and counsellor in the case of ethical dilemmas that arise in counsellors). It consists of the following stages:

1. Gain a good understanding of the facts of a situation

a) What are your emotions informing or misinforming you? What are your emotions? Are they appropriate? If not, what would the appropriate emotions be? If they are, then what information do they provide?

Emotion	Strength	Object	Appropriate?	Information
_____	_____	_____	_____	_____
_____	_____	_____	_____	_____
_____	_____	_____	_____	_____

b) What assumptions might you be making?
c) What further information might you need to understand the situation fully?
d) What actually is *your* problem?

2. Gain a good understanding of what really matters in the situation

a) List all the parties involved. What are the rights, duties, virtues and interests of various parties involved?
b) What do the law and, for professional dilemmas, codes of ethics and best practice say?
c) What do your (appropriate) emotions from Stage 1 suggest about what matters?

d) Looking from a different perspective, that of yourself and the other parties in five years' time, what else might matter?

e) What would you like done if you were in the position of the other parties involved?

f) Imagine that you have the power to put an ideal solution into place (ignore practical problems for now). What would it be? Why would this be a good solution – what are the values that are fulfilled if it is carried out?

For everything that seems to matter, we should evaluate its acceptability, relevance and importance. This will give us an overall weighting of how much it matters. We will end up with a specific list of what matters in this situation, and how much it matters, which will be invaluable in helping us make a wise decision.

What seems to matter	*Acceptability*	*Relevance*	*Importance (/5)*
_____	_____	_____	_____
_____	_____	_____	_____
_____	_____	_____	_____

3. Think up options creatively in the light of what the situation really is and what matters in the situation

a) Weston's 'Finding the best problem'. Go back to the ideal solution of Stage 3 – what are your constraints? What are the constraints – are all these actual constraints? How might they be overcome?

b) Covey's 'win–win' solution. Try to 'breed' options into more successful ones by combining features which meet ethical objectives.

4. Evaluate options

Progress logically suggests that each of the possible courses of action be evaluated in terms of what was found to matter at Stage 3.

Objective	Objective 1	Objective 2	Objective 3	Total
Option				
Option 1	Yes/No/?			
Option 2				
Option 3				
Option 4				

5. Carry out the best option

a) What obstacles might there be to implementing this solution? How can these be overcome?

b) If they cannot be overcome, what might be a fallback solution?

Progress is illustrated by the example of Linda's decision about taking on a couple for counselling on pages 65–72. Further examples can be found on the progress website, http://www.decision-making.co.uk.

The philosophical methods of CBT[12]

Cognitive–behavioural therapy (CBT) is in part a philosophical therapy aimed at identifying and correcting errors in thinking which lead to emotional disturbances. The CBT literature (e.g. Beck, Blackburn and Burns) includes lists of such errors and their remedies which are intended to be taught to clients. Clients are taught both these lists and ways to monitor their automatic thoughts, to which these remedies should be applied (see Burns and Blackburn). They are used in three key ways – to tackle automatic thoughts after and, if possible, during the emotional episode and also to tackle disruptive *core beliefs* which underlie the thoughts. There follow two lists – first a fairly standard list of 'errors in thinking' gleaned from CBT sources, and then a philosophically enhanced list of ways to deal with these errors.

Errors in thinking

Overgeneralizing

Overgeneralizing occurs whenever someone says that something happens all the time when it only happens some of the time, e.g. 'I never have any self-control.'

Personalizing and blame

Personalizing is taking too much blame; the converse is taking too little responsibility and blaming someone else. For example, if my car is vandalized, personalizing would mean saying 'I'm such an idiot for leaving it outside' whereas the blaming response would be 'Why didn't you warn me of vandals in the area?'

Black and white thinking

Black and white thinking is 'either/or' reasoning, not allowing for degrees, categorizing everything at an extreme, e.g. 'I've blown my diet completely.'

Jumping to conclusions

Jumping to conclusions happens when you reach a conclusion without sufficient evidence. Cognitive therapists identify two categories: fortune-telling, when one is drawing conclusions about the future on inadequate evidence (e.g. 'I'm going to fail my exam') and mind-reading, when one is inferring what other people think (e.g. 'She's going to think I'm an idiot').

Catastrophizing and labelling

Catastrophizing is magnifying how bad something is, getting it out of proportion, e.g. 'It will be a disaster if I lose my job.' Allied to catastrophizing is the activity of labelling – either yourself or the event – in excessively negative terms, e.g. 'I'm an idiot.'

Disqualifying the positive and mental filter

This happens when people either don't notice positive things (the mental filter) or else do notice them but play down their significance. For example, suppose you pay me a compliment that I have lost weight. Disqualifying the positive would mean either saying 'You are only saying this to be nice' or perhaps even twisting it into a negative: 'Oh dear, I must be fat if he's commenting on my weight.' The mental filter might happen in the job situation; I ignore the fact that I was chosen for an interview and focus on the fact that I didn't get the job.

'Should' and 'Ought' statements

Cognitive therapists tell people to avoid 'should' statements as in 'I should have got the job' or 'I should be earning a good wage by now.'

A philosophical cognitive therapist's ways to correct errors in thinking

Ways to correct the errors in thinking include asking the following questions about each negative thought. This list goes beyond the standard answers given by cognitive therapists, taking in philosophical insights from the rest of this book.

What error applies to this thought?

The first step is to analyse one's thinking. A good start is to look at it in terms of the seven errors in thinking mentioned above; one could broaden this using the fallacies mentioned in the Critical Thinking literature (see for example Warburton, 1996).

Examine the evidence

Look at actual evidence for and against belief and explanations. Turn each piece of evidence into a *reason* for or against whether the belief or explanation is true, and use the Charles Darwin Method to reassess it.

Treat yourself as you would a sympathetic but honest friend

The CBT literature asks you to treat yourself as a sympathetic friend would, as otherwise you may be applying a double standard. The philosophical cognitive therapist would add that you should be honest as well as sympathetic. Rationalizations and wishful thinking are no route to emotional wisdom.

Avoid black and white, all-or-nothing thinking

Instead of thinking something is all good or all bad, try to see how it is somewhere in between. You can be helped to do this by thinking in terms of *probabilities* and *percentages*. For example, instead of saying 'I've failed the exam' and 'I've completely blown my diet', say (for example) 'There's a 50 per cent chance I've failed the exam' and 'I'm 100 calories over my limit today.'

Avoid loaded emotional language

Re-define emotionally loaded language in more neutral, descriptive terms. Philosophers distinguish a word's 'emotive' meaning from its 'descriptive' one, i.e. the facts it states, from the feelings expressed. Try to use words that stick to the facts. For example, instead of saying 'I'm a disgrace' say 'I am disappointed with myself.'

Examine the long-term consequences of emotions, attitudes and behaviour

What are the pros and cons for having particular attitudes, emotions and behaviour? For example, does getting angry actually do you any good? The long-term consequences should be evaluated in terms of one's values (see RSVP) and ethical principles (see Progress).

Be careful about using 'should' and 'ought' statements

As was argued on pages 105–7, it's not true that you should avoid using these terms as some cognitive therapists have suggested. Instead, ask yourself these questions:

1. Is the action you are commending something that the person in question can actually do in this case (remember that 'ought' implies 'can')?
2. Even if at first sight they may have a duty to do something, is there another duty that overrides it in this case?
3. Is the 'ought' a universal law of morality, or just a parental or societal prescription or a personal preference?

In the final analysis, prudential 'shoulds' are best derived from an understanding of one's values (not necessarily just happiness), which can be gained from RSVP. Ethical 'shoulds' can only be evaluated in terms of acceptable ethical theories, or using a decision procedure such as Progress.

Use the Serenity Prayer

The philosophical version of the Serenity Prayer reads:

> Grant me the serenity to accept the things I cannot change;
> Courage to change the things I can (and should);
> and wisdom to know the difference.

The Serenity Prayer tells us one path to emotional wisdom. In particular, it reminds us that even when things are not as we like, our *attitude* to this state of affairs makes all the difference. If we really are helpless, we should adopt serenity (what is the point of suffering?): if we are not, we should use the emotions as information that something needs changing. To tell the difference, we need wisdom, which encompasses the RSVP-type knowledge of our enlightened values, and Aristotelian practical wisdom about the nature of the situation we find ourselves in.

Conclusion

I HOPE TO HAVE SHOWN that philosophy has much
to offer the counsellor. Philosophy's role in assessing
counselling from the safety of an armchair has been demon-
strated by the critique of a number of counselling approaches,
as well as the key concepts of 'autonomy', 'well-being', 'the
meaning of life', 'reason' and 'the emotions'. Philosophy can
also help counsellors faced with dilemmas in their own work, by
informing them about theories of right and wrong, and by sup-
plying procedures to help with decision-making. But the
greatest value of philosophy is, I believe, very practical. Philosophy is most potent in the front line, as it were, providing
counsellors with powerful methods – the counsellor's philosophical toolbox – which can form a significant part of their
repertoire of skills. RSVP, Progress, the Charles Darwin
Method and the rest are the result of the fruitful marriage of
philosophy and counselling.

The advantages to clients from the use of these methods, and
from philosophical approaches to counselling in general, are
manifold. They include the opportunity for greater clarity,
rigour and creativity. I have singled out three benefits that I
believe are most important: enlightened values, emotional
wisdom and good decisions. I hope that this book helps
stimulate the development of values-focused counselling,
emotion-focused counselling and decision counselling to
promote each of them. A really wise counsellor – someone with
the theoretical wisdom of Socrates, the practical wisdom of

Aristotle, and the empathy of Carl Rogers – will of course do even more than promote enlightened values, emotional wisdom and good decisions in isolation. The ultimate reward for the client is a better chance to lead a more satisfying and meaningful life – no small thing. If counselling accepts all that philosophy has to offer, it can then, and only then, offer such wise therapy.

Postscript:
The existentialist greyhound *or* Jean-Paul Sartre goes to the White City (and loses all his money)[13] (with apologies to P. G. Wodehouse)

It was one of those Saturday nights between the Boat Race and the Lords' Test when Yours Truly was at something of a loose end. Out of the b., Pongo Twistleton rang me to say that he and his Uncle Fred were going to the dog track that night, and would we care to join them? Well, as the poet said, you only live once, so off we toddled to the jolly old White City.

As it happened, Jeeves had invited a couple of French chums over for the weekend – cheerful chaps, ate lots of fish, so they came with us. Pongo's Uncle Fred got us all in for nothing by claiming they were visiting French diplomats, he and Jeeves were members of the Cabinet, and me and Pongo were their assistants. Not a bad start, eh what?

Everything was going swimmingly until after the first race. Then all of a sudden one of the French coves, Albert 'the Cat' Camus, came over in what seemed to young Bertram like a fit of hysterics. 'Mad dogs and Englishmen! I always thought that this country was strange, with your ridiculous pinned-stripe suits and your fox-taunting and inedible chips and fish. But now I see that even the animals are mad in this country. How can they chase after a hare that isn't real, even though they never catch it, week after week? It is unbelievable!'

The other French chappie, Jean-Paul, 'George and Ringo' Sartre, joined in the attack.

'Mon Dieu, you are right, Albert. They all have the free will to make no exit from the starting trap, but they do not use it. They are in bad faith – a bit like that waiter over there . . .'

'Well steady on, old beans,' I interrupted. The Woosters can get quite stirred when the old Mother C's honour is at stake. 'I mean, eh what, steady on!'

As usual, the sharp intellect of young Bertram stopped them in their tracks.

'In fact, Jean-Paul – isn't life one big dog race?' continued Camus excitedly. 'Aren't we all like those poor greyhounds? Don't *we* seek things like happiness and meaning which we can never get? And don't we still keep trying for them?'

After that there was no stopping them, all night. I didn't catch much of the rest, but I think it was all about Exi-something and the myth of Sissy-somebody-else. To be honest it all went a teeny bit over young Bertram's head, but Jeeves seemed most interested – so much so he was no b. help at all picking the winners.

Time passed, and Dame Fortune continued to give us a wide berth. Jeeves seemed unusually agitated though. 'I do believe, sir, that we may have witnessed tonight some developments in the field of philosophy that will not go unnoticed,' he remarked.

'Never mind Phil O'Whatsit and his field – who is going to win the last race?' I bellowed, slightly irritably, trying to turn his attention to more pressing concerns.

'I will endeavour to discover the solution to your conundrum, sir,' he replied, and shimmered off.

Meanwhile Uncle Fred was telling anyone who would listen that he had a hot tip for trap 6, who rejoiced in the name of 'Freddie's Superman.' Pongo and Sartre were both persuaded to put their hard-earned on it, though Camus insisted on betting the outsider.

Just in the nick of time I managed to find Jeeves. 'Put this on Freddie's Superman,' I shouted, handing him next year's subscription to the Drones.

'Very good, sir, if that is sir's wish.'

Well, blow me but trap 6 ran as if it was my Aunt Agatha,

while trap 1 ran as if it had Aunt Agatha chasing it. A few minutes later, to my great surprise and delight, Jeeves handed me a large bundle of notes, as juicy as one of Anatole's steaks.

'I thought I told you to bet trap 6!'

'Yes, sir, you did. But I chanced upon Lord Russell's butler on the way to the bookmakers. His lordship, you understand, is connected with the winning greyhound. He conveyed to me the suggestion that an investment in trap 1 might in the long run transpire to be the more prudent option.'

On the way home I couldn't stop beaming to myself. I kept asking everyone to confirm my feeling that everything was indeed for the best in the best of all possible worlds. Unfortunately this seemed to make Camus and Sartre even more miserable. They seemed totally transformed – couldn't get a laugh out of them all the way home. According to Jeeves, they never ever recovered their previous *bon viveur*. And all because of one of Uncle Fred's lousy tips. Funny old world, eh what?

Notes

Chapter 1

1 This is not to deny that *other* people who are severely depressed or anxious may benefit from diagnosis and medication.

2 Throughout this book, as is common (but not universal) practice in the UK, I use the words 'therapy' and 'counselling' synonymously.

3 Critical thinking is sometimes referred to as 'informal logic' or 'critical reasoning'.

4 Phenomenologists are however interested in a person's reasons, which makes the 'Why?' question very tempting. A question like 'Why are you so upset by your husband?' is just as likely to get a response in terms of causes ('I was really tired after looking after the baby all day') as reasons ('It's wrong that he should stay out drinking all night'). So it is important to rephrase such questions explicitly in terms of reasons, e.g. 'What are your reasons for being so upset by your husband's behaviour?'

5 The case vignette of Claire (pp. 73–7) illustrates an example of the Life Design in action.

6 Utilitarianism is explored in more detail in Chapter 2.

7 It should not necessarily be inferred that the more philosophical an approach is, the better. Whether or not an approach is better depends both on the philosophical question of whether its aims are worthwhile, and the empirical question of whether it actually achieves its aims.

8 Plato's earlier dialogues (Charmides, Crito, Euthydemus, Euthyphro, Gorgias, Hippias Major, Hippias Minor, Ion, Laches, Lysis, Menexenus, Meno, Protagoras, Republic I) are more normally taken to be attempts to recapture Socrates' own philosophy; in the later dialogues Plato increasingly uses Socrates as a mouthpiece for his own views.

9 See the resources section on p. 185 for details.

10 A version of this case vignette first appeared in *Humanity* (14: February/March 2000), Newsletter of the British Humanist Association.

11 Socrates himself imposed a method, the *elenchus*, on clients.

12 There are many cognitive and behavioural therapies, which makes terminology confusing. I reserve the term CBT to talk about the (mainly

cognitive) therapy invented by Beck, and REBT to refer to Rational Emotive Behavioural Therapy associated with Ellis and Dryden. When talking more generally, I use the term 'cognitive therapy'.

Part 1

1 God, it might be answered in reply, is not any old authority. God would only command us to do things that really are good, because God himself is good. But then we need to ask what the statement 'God is good' amounts to. If it is saying anything more than that God approves of God, it must be saying that goodness depends on other things, which leads us back into the horns of the dilemmas posed in *Euthyphro*.

2 These mistaken types of relativism are not to be confused with the correct theory which says that what we should do is relative to the situation; these theories say that what we should do is relative to the person or society.

3 The qualifications 'simply' and 'straightforwardly' are very important here. One major modern theory about ethical statements, moral realism, states that ethical statements are in some sense matters of fact. We will in fact be endorsing Michael Smith's realist view.

4 More precisely, 'strong' versions of relativism and emotivism overstate their case. 'Weak' versions, which allow for a place for reason in ethics, are not necessarily guilty of this mistake.

5 A second historical benefit of the emotive theory was that it led to theorists paying more attention to 'the language of morals', which is actually the title of an important book by R. M. Hare which was influenced by, but argued against, the emotivist's view.

6 Note that giving a reason is very different from identifying a cause, although this is often blurred since we use the word 'because' in both cases. Reasons are grounds for doing or believing something; they are meant to convince us; causes are merely an historical fact which has led to something. In ethics we justify choices by giving reasons, not by identifying causes.

Chapter 2

1 The position under discussion is sometimes referred to as *ethical* hedonism – the view that all we ought to pursue is our own pleasure. This is to distinguish it from another (false) view called *psychological hedonism*, which is the view that all we in fact pursue is our own pleasure.

2 This is not to take sides in the debate over whether states of mind are, ultimately, the only things that matter. The Cambridge philosopher G. E. Moore thought that a world containing one beautiful object but no people would be good. He thought that there are some states of the world that are good or bad completely independently of states of mind. But the distinction between states of mind and states of the world does not rely on this.

3 Interestingly, some people respond that they would like to save up their time in the Experience Machine for when they are very ill or old. This sug-

gests that happiness may become more of a priority when we are in pain, or incapable of achieving any changes to the world. However Freud, famously, refused pain-killers in the last days of his life as he preferred the ability to think to a pain-free life without the ability to think clearly.

4   The term 'Objective List theories' is used instead by some writers, including James Griffin and Derek Parfit. A value is something whose fulfilment we take to be a good thing, other things being equal; objective theories say these are objective, others disagree.

5   These values are chosen for being interesting rather than for being examples of 'objective' theorists; of the three Finnis is the only clear objectivist.

6   Plato's theory of the Forms has been roundly criticized by nearly all commentators, from Plato's pupil Aristotle onwards. Yet its influence – partly through its absorption into Judeo–Christian thought where it is expressed in terms of God and heaven – is immense.

7   They are also sometimes called 'intrinsic preferences'. Kekes (1988) calls them 'ideals'.

8   It would be technically correct to group informed and rational preferences together, since fully rational preferences will also be well-informed ones. I chose to describe the two criteria separately because of the importance of well-informed desires which are nonetheless irrational because of the strength of the desire and the failure to take future desires into account properly.

9   A difference between IPT and totally objective theories is that IPT still leaves open the possibility that you and I might have different lists of values. It is an empirical question whether the values people come up with when they think through their values in ideal conditions are similar to each other. As we shall see, RSVP is a method for coming up with such a list. It would be fascinating to compare different lists of the values generated by RSVP.

10   The view that emotions can be irrational as well will be argued for in Chapter 4.

11   Crumbaugh uses the term 'logoanalysis' to differentiate it from the more psychiatric logotherapy.

12   One road this can take the existentialist down is that of making authenticity an overriding value, which, on one interpretation of authenticity, makes it open to Taylor's objections.

13   In philosophical counselling's defence, it could be argued that Socrates proceeded in the same way, i.e. trying to work out the answers from scratch. At least Socrates had the excuse that he thought that he knew nothing, and also provided a focus (compare with the Socratic method that follows). See also my paper in Curnow, T. (ed.) (2001) for a further discussion of these issues.

14   This vignette is based on an article in *The Philosophers' Magazine* (LeBon, 1999).

Chapter 3

1   Earlier proto-utilitarians include Protagoras and Hume.

2   All these criticisms apply to Benthamite act-utilitarianism. Other forms of utilitarianism, including Mill's and Hare's, can be defended against some – but not all – of them.

3   According to Kant, moral principles are *imperatives*, because they are commands to behave in a specified way, and they are *categorical*, because they must be obeyed in all circumstances, not only when they are in accord with your own or other people's preferences. There are actually several versions of the Categorical Imperative – the one given is known as the 'formula of Universal Law'.

4   Hare suggests that apparent contradictions between the theories are resolved when we realize that they operate at different levels of moral thinking. Hare (1981) argues that there are two levels of moral thinking, the intuitive and the critical. Were we superior creatures with the capacity to do instantaneous reasoning and calculations, and no propensity to favour ourselves, we should try to work out what to do from scratch in each situation we find ourselves in. Utilitarianism's mistake, according to Hare, is to think that we need to operate at this level – the critical level of moral thinking – all the time. In fact, it would be disastrous if we tried to do utilitarian calculations all the time, for all the reasons listed above. Given our limitations, we shall not achieve the best outcome by doing a utilitarian calculation each time. Instead, we should cultivate in ourselves a set of principles which in general lead to the best outcome. These principles will become second nature to us – they are our moral intuitions. At the intuitive level, we behave much like Kantians – sticking to principles and virtues whatever the consequences, and only departing from doing our duty with the greatest reluctance and guilt. Critical reasoning should be used only to select the best set of principles for use in intuitive thinking and to resolve conflicts between principles. Hare thinks that utilitarianism operates at the critical level. His argument for this conclusion, based on a complex conceptual analysis of the moral words, is not ultimately persuasive (LeBon, 1984). Hare's theory about the two levels of moral thinking means that we can ignore the second set of objections, based on the difficulty of calculating consequences. Our discussion in Chapter 2 helps us base it on well-being rather than pleasure or happiness. Utilitarianism is a much more plausible theory if it is reframed as one which produces a set of virtues and principles to impartially maximize well-being. Yet there is still the suspicion that even modified utilitarianism is too *thin* – it does not capture everything that matters. In particular, concerns that the distribution of well-being and duties to specific people will be underestimated by utilitarianism suggest that we need a procedure at the critical level to take everything that matters ethically into account rather than *just* the maximization of well-being.

5 Weston does not, as far as I am aware, explicitly identify himself as a virtue ethicist. However, his insights into the virtues required to be a skilled ethical decision-maker justify him being classified as such.

6 The theory that perhaps best combines utilitarianism, Kantianism and virtue ethics is that of the twentieth-century Oxford philosopher R. M. Hare. See Note 4 above.

7 I owe the idea of applying critical thinking methodology to decision-making to David Arnaud.

8 The Epicurean idea described on page 35 is in effect enhanced by CDM.

Chapter 4

1 See Damasio (1994) and LeDoux (1999) for lucid accounts of developments in this area.

2 See Lazarus and Lazarus (1994) for a particularly clear introduction to the psychological literature on emotions.

3 If indeed we have no control over tickles, aches and pains.

4 This is not to say that drugs like Prozac work purely physiologically; they may have an effect on mood and cognitions as well.

5 These considerations can be strengthened by arguments about the *logic* of emotional words. For example, the *judgement* that someone has committed a wrong is central to the concept of anger. Without this judgement an emotion would not be called 'anger' – whatever the bodily feeling that occurred.

6 Ryle, as a logical behaviourist philosopher, argues that, conceptually, emotions are *only* dispositions to behave. Skinner and Watson, as behaviourist psychologists, are much more interested in discovering how the manipulation of external stimuli can affect emotions. There is a link between the two; if, as Ryle thinks, emotions are behaviour, then the same principles of learning theory, which apply to behaviour, can also be applied to emotions.

7 Moods too are often, if not always, intentional, e.g. a child sulking about not getting the present he wanted.

8 George Kelly turned this Kantian insight into a whole approach to counselling, Personal Construct Therapy.

9 The Serenity Prayer is of course associated with Alcoholics Anonymous (AA); my point is that it has a much broader application.

10 The downward arrow technique would only be recommended to be carried out by the client themselves with great care, since by definition it can uncover some scary material which the therapist needs to know will be challenged effectively.

11 The Stoics made a distinction between those things that were absolutely good and those things that were merely preferred. They placed most conventional goods (including health and wealth) in the latter category.

12 This also illustrates the point that PC can take any idea as a source for

philosophical discussion, not just those traditionally taught at universities! The contrast between Aristophenes and St Exupéry was suggested to me by an entertaining talk on love given by Peter Rickman to the Society for Existential Analysis.

13 In a response to this suggestion, Cohen states that 'I use critical thinking didactically. I teach clients to recognise many different informal fallacies, and yes, it is effective with clients having the requisite cognitive abilities. As for research to see which fallacies are represented, the most frequently in client thinking, my clinical experience has informed me that this depends upon the client population and is quite variable between individuals. While some generalizations are possible, it is still better to gear didactic counselling to the individual rather than to make assumptions about what regime of logic is best to teach in advance of exploring the individual client's belief system.' (Personal correspondence, 25 October 2000.)

Chapter 5

1 Should Tolstoy and those like him commit suicide on the basis of authenticity rather than nihilism? Personally, I would need a lot of convincing that authenticity is the only positive state of mind or state of the world, i.e. I believe it is one of a plurality of values. But even if one could consistently hold that authenticity is the only value (or perhaps an overriding value), given that nihilism no longer holds, just why is it authentic to commit suicide?

2 But even this subjective meaning is insecure, because we may discover that our life is objectively meaningless. Casaubon might find out that someone else has already found the key.

Chapter 6

1 The technical term 'cogent' is sometimes used instead of 'good' to describe a sound argument.

2 The critical thinking literature also contains a good deal of material about bad arguments, and there are many books which list types of fallacies to be avoided (see for example Warburton (1996) and Thouless (1930)). For example: the 'Fallacy of equivocation' happens when we use ambiguous language so that there are different senses of the same word in a premise and the conclusion.

3 Govier calls the 'Pros and Cons' argument the less obvious name 'conductive'. It is also sometimes called a 'good reasons' type of argument.

4 In particular see Govier (1992), Thomson (1999) and Johnson and Blair (1994).

5 These three criteria apply to all the types of argument mentioned ('Pros and Cons' arguments, arguments from analogy, inductive and deductive arguments) and are particularly helpful when dealing with 'Pros and

Cons' arguments.

6   The particular criteria given for rationality are my own, adapted for the purposes of counselling. For a somewhat more complex account, see Govier (1992).

7   As we shall see, moral statements are partly a matter of evaluation as well as fact, therefore the criterion 'acceptability' may be preferable to 'truth' when discussing moral statements.

8   This might actually be false, if computer programs like Eliza are considered to be counsellors!

9   This method owes much to John Wilson in *Thinking with Concepts*. See also Chapter 6 of Philip Cam's *Thinking Together: Philosophical Inquiry for the Classroom*. Note that the term 'concept' is used rather than 'word' because it applies to words (e.g. autonomy) and phrases (e.g. 'meaning of life').

10 RSVP stands for 'Refined Subjective Value Procedure'. My thanks to all those who have helped improve RSVP, including Antonia Macaro, Bill Anderson, Shamil Chandaria and David Arnaud.

11 Progress was developed by David Arnaud, Tim LeBon and Antonia Macaro.

12 The list of errors in thinking are a composite of Burns (1990) and Blackburn (1987).

13 I would like to thank Alan Harlow for suggesting this title. A different version of this piece first appeared in *Philosophy Now*.

Bibliography and References

Aristotle (various) *Nicomachean Ethics* (trans. W. D. Ross).

Arnaud, D. and LeBon, T. (2000) *Towards Wise Decision-Making in Practical Philosophy.* London: SCP.

Arnaud, D., LeBon, T. and Macaro, A. (2000) *Progress: A Procedure for Wise Decision-making*, on www at http://www.decision-making.co.uk.

Beck, A. (1976/1991) *Cognitive Therapy and the Emotional Disorders.* London: Penguin.

Bentham, J. (1948/1789) *Introduction to the Principles of Morals and Legislation.* New York: Hafner.

Blackburn, I. (1987) *Coping with Depression.* Edinburgh: Chambers.

Bloch, S., Chodoff, P. and Green, S. A. (1999) *Psychiatric Ethics.* Oxford: OUP.

Bond, T. (2000) *Standards and Ethics for Counselling in Action.* London: Sage.

Burkhardt, F. and Smith, S. (ed.) (1986) *The Correspondence of Charles Darwin, Vol. 2.* Cambridge: CUP.

Burns, D. (1990) *The Feeling Good Handbook.* London: Penguin.

Calhoun, C. and Solomon, R. (1984) *What Is an Emotion?: Classic Readings in Philosophical Psychology.* Oxford: OUP.

Cam, P. (1995) *Thinking Together: Philosophical Inquiry for the Classroom.* Sydney: Hale and Iremonger.

Camus, A. (1942/1975) *The Myth of Sisyphus.* London: Penguin.

Cohen, E. (1992) *Caution: Faulty Thinking Can Be Harmful to Your Happiness.* Fort Pierce, Florida: Trace-Wilco.

Cohen, E. (1995) 'Philosophical counselling: some roles of critical thinking', in R. Lahav and M. Tillmans, *Essays on Philosophical Counselling.* Lanham: University Press of America.

Cohen, E. and Cohen, G. (1999) *The Virtuous Therapist.* Belmont, CA: Brooks/Cole.

Cohn, H. W. (1997) *Existential Thought and Therapeutic Practice.* London: Sage.

Covey, S. (1992) *The Seven Habits of Highly Effective People.* London: Simon and Schuster.

Crumbaugh, J. (1973) *Everything to Gain.* Berkeley, CA: Institute of Logotherapy Press.

Culley, S. (1990) *Integrative Counselling Skills in Action.* London: Sage.

Curnow, T. (ed.) (2001) *Thinking Through Dialogue: Essays on Philosophy in*

Practice. London: SCP.

Damasio, A. (1994) *Descartes' Error.* New York: MacMillan.

Dawkins, R. (1976) *The Selfish Gene.* Oxford: OUP.

de Bono, E. (1982) *de Bono's Thinking Course.* London: BBC.

de Botton, A. (2000) *The Consolations of Philosophy.* London: Hamish Hamilton.

Deurzen, E. van (1999) 'Common sense or nonsense: intervening in moral dilemmas', in *British Journal of Guidance and Counselling,* Vol. 27, No. 4.

Deurzen-Smith, E. van (1988) *Existential Counselling in Practice.* London: Sage.

Deurzen-Smith, E. van (1990) 'Existential therapy', in W. Dryden (ed.) *Individual Therapy.* Oxford: OUP.

Deurzen-Smith, E. van (1994) *Can Counselling Help?* Durham: School of Education, University of Durham.

Deurzen-Smith, E. van (1997) *Everyday Mysteries – Existential Dimensions of Psychotherapy.* London: Routledge.

Deurzen-Smith, E. van (1998) *Paradox and Passion in Psychotherapy.* Chichester: Wiley.

Dryden, W. (1995) *Brief Rational Emotive Behaviour Therapy.* Chichester: Wiley.

du Plock, S. (ed.) (1997) *Case Studies in Existential Psychotherapy and Counselling.* Chichester: Wiley.

du Plock, S. (1999) 'On dialogue between philosophical counselling and existential psychotherapy', in *Journal of the Society for Existential Analysis,* Vol. 10, No. 1.

Egan, G. (1990) *The Skilled Helper.* Belmont, CA: Brooks/Cole.

Ellis, A. (1962) *Reason and Emotion in Psychotherapy.* New York: Birch Lane Press.

Elster, J. (1999) *Alchemies of the Mind: Rationality and the Emotions.* Cambridge: CUP.

Feltham, C. and Dryden, W. (1993) *Dictionary of Counselling.* London: Whurr.

Finnis, J. (1980) *Natural Law and Natural Rights.* Oxford: Clarendon Press.

Fleming, J. (2000) 'Wisdom and virtue in philosophical counselling', in *Practical Philosophy,* Vol. 3, No. 1. London: SCP.

Frankl, V. (1946/1959) *Man's Search for Meaning.* London: Hodder and Stoughton.

Frankl, V. (1965) *The Doctor and the Soul.* New York: Bantam Books.

Frankl, V. (1985) *The Unheard Cry for Meaning: Psychotherapy and Humanism.* New York: Simon and Schuster.

Gaarder, J. (1995) *Sophie's World.* London: Phoenix.

Govier, T. (1992) *A Practical Study of Argument.* Belmont, CA: Wadsworth.

Griffin, J. (1986) *Well-being.* Oxford: OUP.

Hammond, J., Keeney, R. and Raiffa, H. (1999) *Smart Choices.* Boston, MA: HBS Press.

Hare, R. M. (1952) *Freedom and Reason.* Oxford: OUP.

Hare, R. M. (1963) *The Language of Morals.* Oxford: OUP.

Hare, R. M. (1981) *Moral Thinking.* Oxford: Clarendon Press.

Hare, R. M. (1997) *Sorting Out Ethics.* Oxford: Clarendon Press.

Holmes, J. and Lindley, R. (1991) *The Values of Psychotherapy.* Oxford: OUP.

Honderich, T. (ed.) (1995) *The Oxford Companion to Philosophy*. Oxford: OUP.

Hoogendijk, A. (1995) 'The philosopher in the business world as a vision developer', in R. Lahav and M. Tillmans, *Essays on Philosophical Counselling*. Lanham: University Press of America.

Howard, A. (2000) *Philosophy for Counselling and Psychotherapy*. Basingstoke: Macmillan.

Inwood, B. and Gerson, L. P. (1994) *The Epicurus Reader: Selected Writings and Testimonia*. Indianapolis/Cambridge: Hackett.

Inwood, M. (1997) *Heidegger*. Oxford: OUP.

James, W. (1948) *Psychology*. New York: World Publishing.

Johnson, R. H. and Blair, J. Anthony (1994) *Logical Self-defense*. New York: McGraw Hill.

Kant, I. (1785/1948) *Groundwork of the Metaphysics of Morals*. London: Routledge.

Kekes, J. (1992) *The Examined Life*. Pennsylvania: Pennsylvania State University Press.

Klemke, E. D. (ed.) (1981) *The Meaning of Life*. New York: OUP.

Klinger, E. (1977) *Meaning and Void: Inner Experiences and the Incentives in People's Lives*. Minneapolis: University of Minnesota Press.

Kupperman, J. (1999) *Value . . . and What Follows*. New York: OUP.

Lahav, R. (1993) 'Using analytic philosophy in counselling', in *Journal of Applied Philosophy*, Vol. 10, No. 2, pp. 243–53.

Lahav, R. (1995) 'A conceptual framework for philosophical counselling: worldview interpretation', in R. Lahav and M. Tillmans, *Essays on Philosophical Counselling*. Lanham: University Press of America.

Lahav, R. (1998) 'On the possibility of a dialogue between philosophical counselling and existential psychotherapy', in *Journal of the Society for Existential Analysis*, Vol. 9, No. 1, pp. 129–44.

Lahav, R. and Tillmans, M. (1995) *Essays on Philosophical Counselling*. Lanham: University Press of America.

Law, S. (2000) *The Philosophy Files*. London: Dolphin.

Lazarus, R. and Lazarus, B. (1994) *Passion and Reason: Making Sense of Our Emotions*. Oxford: OUP.

LeBon, T. (1984) 'Hare's Moral Thinking: A Critique' (M.Phil. dissertation for London University).

LeBon, T. (1994) 'The existentialist greyhound', in *Philosophy Now*, Issue 9.

LeBon, T. (1999/2000) 'The clinic' series, in *The Philosophers' Magazine*.

LeBon, T. (2000) '6 months to live', in *Humanity*, Issue 14.

LeBon, T. (2001a) 'Philosophical counselling: an introduction', in T. Curnow (ed.) *Thinking Through Dialogue: Proceedings of the 6th International Conference on Philosophy in Practice*. London: SCP.

LeBon, T. (2001b) 'Socrates, philosophical counselling and thinking through dialogue', in T. Curnow (ed.) *Thinking Through Dialogue: Proceedings of the 6th International Conference on Philosophy in Practice*. London: SCP.

LeDoux, J. (1999) *The Emotional Brain*. London: The Phoenix Press.

Mace, C. (ed.) (1999) *Heart and Soul: The Therapeutic Face of Philosophy*. London: Routledge.

Mackie, J. (1977) *Ethics: Inventing Right and Wrong*. London: Penguin.

Marinoff, L. (1998) Interview by Tim LeBon in *Philosophy Now*, 20, Spring, pp. 7–10.

Marinoff, L. (1999) *Plato Not Prozac!* New York: Harper Collins.

Mill, J. S. (1861/1979) *Utilitarianism*. Glasgow: Collins.

Morton, A. (1996) *Philosophy in Practice*. Oxford: Blackwell.

Nagel, T. (1979) *Mortal Questions*. Cambridge: CUP.

Nagel, T. (1987) *What Does It All Mean?* New York: OUP.

Newcomb, M. D. and Harlow, L. L. (1986) 'Life events and substance abuse among adolescents: mediating effects of perceived loss of control and meaninglessness in life', in *Journal of Personality and Social Psychology*, 51, pp. 564–77.

Nisbett, R. and Ross, L. (1980) *Human Inference: Strategies and Shortcomings of Social Judgement*. New Jersey: Prentice-Hall.

Nozick, R. (1974) *Anarchy, State and Utopia*. Oxford: Blackwell.

Paden, R. (1998) 'Defining philosophical counselling', in *International Journal of Applied Philosophy*, Vol. 12, No. 1.

Plato (various) *Euthyphro*. London: Penguin Classics.

Plato (various) *The Republic*. London: Penguin Classics.

Plato (1969) *The Apology*. London: Penguin Classics.

Plato (1987) *Early Socratic Dialogues*. London: Penguin Classics.

Popper, K. (1977) 'How I see philosophy', in A. Mercier and M. Svilar (eds) *Philosophers in Their Own Work, Vol. 3*. New York: Peter Lang.

Raabe, P. (2001) *Philosophical Counseling: Theory and Practice*. Westport, CT: Praeger.

Rachels, J. (1999) *The Elements of Moral Philosophy*. New York: McGraw-Hill College.

Rescher, N. (1988) *Rationality*. Oxford: Clarendon.

Robertson, D. (1998) 'Philosophical and counter-philosophical practice', in *Practical Philosophy* (Journal of the Society of Consultant Philosophers), December.

Robertson, D. (2000) 'REBT, philosophy and philosophical counselling', in *Practical Philosophy*, Vol. 3, No. 3.

Robinson, R. (1964) *An Atheist's Values*. Oxford: Blackwell.

Ruschmann, E. (1998) 'Foundations of philosophical counselling', in *Inquiry*, Vol. 17, No. 3.

Ryle, G. (1949) *The Concept of Mind*. London: Penguin.

Sartre, J. P. (1939/1962) *The Emotions: A Sketch of a Theory*. London: Routledge.

Sartre, J. P. (1958) *Being and Nothingness*. London: Routledge.

Sartre, J. P. (1997) *Essays in Existentialism*. Secaucus, NJ: Citadel.

Scarre, G. (1996) *Utilitarianism*. London: Routledge.

Schuster, S. C. (1999) *Philosophy Practice: An Alternative to Counselling and Psychotherapy*. Westport, CT: Praeger.

Scruton, R. (1997) 'The return of the sophist', in *The Times*. London, 11 August.

Shibles, W. (1998) 'Philosophical counselling, philosophical education and emotion', in *International Journal of Applied Philosophy*, Vol. 12, No. 1.

Singer, P. (1979) *Practical Ethics*. Cambridge: CUP.

Singer, P. (1994) *How Are We to Live?* London: Mandarin.

Singer, P. (ed.) (1994) *Ethics: The Oxford Reader*. Oxford: OUP.

Skinner, B. and Holland, J. (1961) *The Analysis of Behaviour*. New York: McGraw-Hill.

Smith, M. (1994) 'Realism', in P. Singer (ed.) *Ethics: The Oxford Reader*. Oxford: OUP.

Solomon, R. C. (1993) *The Passions*. Indianapolis/Cambridge: Hackett.

Sorabji, R. (2000) *Emotions and Peace of Mind*. Oxford: OUP.

Spinelli, E. (1989) *The Interpreted World: An Introduction to Phenomenological Psychology*. London: Sage.

Spinelli, E. (1996) *Demystifying Therapy*. London: Constable.

Spinelli, E. (1997) *Tales of Un-knowing*. London: Duckworth.

Stevenson, L. and Haberman, D. (1998) *Ten Theories of Human Nature*. Oxford: OUP.

Strasser, F. (1999) *Emotions: Experiences in Existential Psychotherapy and Life*. London: Duckworth.

Strasser, F. and Strasser, A. (1997) *Existential Time-Limited Therapy*. Chichester: Wiley.

Sumner, L. (1996) *Welfare, Happiness and Ethics*. Oxford: OUP.

Sutherland, S. (1992) *Irrationality*. London: Penguin.

Taylor, C. (1991) *The Ethics of Authenticity*. Cambridge, MA: Harvard University Press.

Thomson, A. (1999) *Critical Reasoning in Ethics*. London: Routledge.

Thouless, R. H. (1930) *Straight and Crooked Thinking*. London: Pan.

Tolstoy, L. (1905) *My Confession*, trans. L. Wiener. London: J. M. Dent & Sons.

Walen, S., diGiuseppe, R. and Wessler, R. (1980) *A Practitioner's Guide to Rational-Emotive Therapy*. New York: OUP.

Warburton, N. (1991) *Philosophy: The Basics*. London: Routledge.

Warburton, N. (1996) *Thinking from A to Z*. London: Routledge.

Warburton, N. (1998) *Philosophy: The Classics*. London: Routledge.

Weston, A. (1992) *A Rulebook for Arguments*. Indianapolis/Cambridge: Hackett.

Weston, A. (1997) *A Practical Companion to Ethics*. New York: OUP.

Wilson, J. (1969) *Thinking with Concepts*. Cambridge: CUP.

Wittgenstein, L. (1921) *Tractatus Logico-Philosophicus*, trans. D. Pears and B. McGuiness. London: Routledge and Kegan Paul.

Wong, P. and Fry, P. (1998) *The Human Quest for Meaning*. Mahway, New Jersey: LEA.

Woolfolk, R. (2000) 'Cognition and emotion in counselling and psychotherapy', in *Practical Philosophy*, Vol. 3, No. 3.

Yalom, I. (1980) *Existential Psychotherapy*. New York: Basic Books.

Yalom, I. (1989) *Love's Executioner*. London: Penguin.

Yalom, I. (1999) *Momma and the Meaning of Life*. London: Piatkus.

Recommended Reading

General introductions to philosophy

Nigel Warburton's *Philosophy: The Basics* and *Philosophy: The Classics* are lucid and well-written introductions from a thematic and historical perspective respectively. Thomas Nagel's *What Does It All Mean?* is shorter, and very good. Stephen Law's *The Philosophy Files* is meant for children, but contains a better introduction to key issues than most books aimed at adults. Stevenson and Haberman's *Ten Theories of Human Nature* is very well structured, and includes chapters on Sartre and Plato. Ted Honderich's *The Oxford Companion to Philosophy* is perhaps the best reference book available. Of course, Plato's dialogues remain one of the best introductions to philosophy – *Euthyphro, Meno, Symposium* and *The Republic* being good ones to start with.

Philosophical counselling

Essays on Philosophical Counselling (edited by Lahav and Tillmans) remains the seminal work on philosophical counselling. *Thinking Through Dialogue: Essays on Philosophy in Practice* (edited by Trevor Curnow) provides a more up-to-date survey of the field and includes not only many papers on philosophical counselling but also covers philosophy in education and business.

Lou Marinoff's *Plato Not Prozac!* includes a presentation of many cases in the manner of a self-help book. Shlomit Schuster's *Philosophy Practice: An Alternative to Counselling and Psychotherapy* is a more academic treatment; as the title suggests, Schuster is less sympathetic to psychological models of counselling than the present writer. Peter Raabe's *Philosophical Counseling: Theory and Practice* came out as this book went to press, and is written by one of the leading writers on the subject. David Lodge's novel *Therapy* is recommended both as an entertaining novel about the contemporary 'therapy-culture' and also as a description of how philosophy – in this case Kierkegaard – can be of practical importance.

Existential–phenomenological counselling

Emmy van Deurzen Smith's *Existential Counselling in Practice* and Irvin Yalom's *Existential Psychotherapy* are two classics in the field. Yalom's *Momma and the Meaning of Life* and *Love's Executioner* and Ernesto Spinelli's *Tales of Unknowing* show how it works in practice. Strasser and Strasser's *Existential Time-Limited Therapy* is a coherent synthesis of existential ideas. Michael Inwood's *Heidegger* is recommended as an introduction to Heidegger; Sartre's *Essays in Existentialism* is a good collection of Sartre's works.

Cognitive therapy

Aaron Beck's *Cognitive Therapy and the Emotional Disorders* remains a good overview of CBT, Albert Ellis's *Reason and Emotion in Psychotherapy* of REBT. However, David Burns' *The Feeling Good Handbook* is perhaps the best introduction to cognitive therapy. The works of Windy Dryden are also recommended, as is his *Individual Therapy in Britain* which provides an excellent overview of counselling as a whole in the UK.

Logotherapy

Frankl's *Man's Search for Meaning* is a good introduction to Frankl and logotherapy, Crumbaugh's *Everything to Gain* is hard to obtain, but very good.

Philosophy in practice

Alain de Botton's *The Consolations of Philosophy* is a very well-written book about the practical application of the ideas of six philosophers, including Seneca, Epicurus, Socrates and Nietzsche. Alex Howard's *Philosophy for Counselling and Psychotherapy* provides an historical account of the major philosophers and their connection with counselling.

General counselling skills

Of many books, Sue Culley's *Integrative Counselling Skills in Action* and Gerald Egan's *The Skilled Helper* are among the best.

Part 1: Ethics

Peter Singer's *Ethics: The Oxford Reader* is an indispensable collection of essays. J. Mackie's *Ethics: Inventing Right and Wrong* is a classic, if somewhat partisan, account of metaethics.

Chapter 2

James Griffin's *Well-being* is a classic, if difficult, survey of ideas about well-being. John Kekes' *The Examined Life* is an excellent, easy-to-read book, to which I owe much. Richard Robinson's *An Atheist's Values* is a third book which I found very useful. Holmes and Lindley's *The Values of Psychotherapy* attempts to defend therapy in terms of autonomy and is very well written.

Chapter 3

Aristotle's *Nicomachean Ethics* remains the classic work of virtue ethics and is very easy to read, if rather dry. S. Covey's *The Seven Habits of Highly Effective People* is a modern, American neo-Aristotelian self-help book. *de Bono's Thinking Course* is one of many books where the lateral thinking master explains his ideas. Peter Singer's *Practical Ethics* is a modern utilitarian treatment of practical issues, Geoffrey Scarre's *Utilitarianism* is a thorough and readable treatment. J. S. Mill's *Utilitarianism* is still well worth reading. R. M. Hare's *Moral Thinking* provides the mature philosophy of one of the leading moral philosophers of the twentieth century. Anthony Weston's *A Practical Companion to Ethics* is both easy to read and an enjoyable read, and much recommended. Anne Thomson's *Critical Reasoning in Ethics* is also very useful. Hammond *et al.*'s *Smart Choices* provides a self-help and sophisticated account of decision-making. Tim Bond's *Standards and Ethics for Counselling in Action* is a solid and reliable guide to counselling ethics in the UK. Elliot and Gale Cohen's *The Virtuous Therapist* has the added virtue of being written jointly by a philosopher and a counsellor, and has a North American perspective.

Chapter 4

Calhoun and Solomon's *What Is an Emotion?* is a very useful collection of short philosophical essays on the emotions. Solomon's classic *The Passions* is a readable account of his own ideas. Lazarus and Lazarus's *Passion and Reason: Making Sense of Our Emotions* is a good psychological overview of theories. Richard Sorabji's *Emotions and Peace of Mind* is a masterful account of philosophy and the emotions from the Stoics to St Augustine. Freddie Strasser's *Emotions: Experiences in Existential Psychotherapy and Life* contains an existentialist perspective. Nisbett and Ross's *Human Inference: Strategies and Shortcomings of Social Judgement* is a classic on the sort of cognitive mistakes people can make. Stuart Sutherland's *Irrationality* is a less academic treatment and Nicholas Rescher's *Rationality* a philosophical overview. The November 2000 edition of *Practical Philosophy* is a special edition devoted to reason, the emotions and philosophy in practice.

Chapter 5

The Meaning of Life (edited by Klemke) is an invaluable collection, containing essays by Tolstoy, Camus and Hare.

Chapter 6

Johnson and Blair's *Logical Self-defense*, Trudy Govier's *A Practical Study of Argument*, Nigel Warburton's *Thinking from A to Z* and Anthony Weston's *A Rulebook for Arguments* are all recommended. John Wilson's *Thinking with Concepts* is one of a small number of books actually telling you how to do conceptual analysis.

Resources

Websites

Site	Address
British Humanist Association	http://www.humanism.org.uk
New School of Psychotherapy & Counselling	http://www.nspc.org.uk
Philosophical Society of England	http://www.philsoc.co.uk
Philosophy Now	http://www.philosophynow.demon.co.uk
Practical Philosophy	http://www.practical-philosophy.org.uk
Progress decision procedure	http://www.decision-making.co.uk
Society of Consultant Philosophers	http://www.society-of-consultant-philosophers.org.uk
Society for Existential Analysis	http://www.existential.mcmail.com
The Philosophers' Magazine (TPM)	http://www.philosophers.co.uk
The School of Psychotherapy and Counselling at Regent's College	http://www.spc.ac.uk
The Stoic Foundation	http://members.aol.com/cyberstoic
Tim LeBon's site (includes information on this book)	http://members.aol.com/timlebon

E-mails/phone numbers

Name/Organization	E-mail/telephone
British Humanist Association	members@humanism.org.uk
New School of Psychotherapy & Counselling	admin@nspc.org.uk
Philosophical Society of England	thephilosophicalsociety@yahoo.co.uk
Philosophy Now	rick.lewis@philosophynow.demon.co.uk
Practical Philosophy	editor@practical-philosophy.org.uk

Progress decision procedure
  (decision counselling and training)   davidarnau@aol.com
                                         amacaro@aol.com
                                         timlebon@aol.com
Society of Consultant Philosophers   enquiries@society-of-consultant-
                                         philosophers.org.uk
Society for Existential Analysis   exist@cwmcom.net
The Philosophers' Magazine (TPM)   editor@philosophers.co.uk
The School of Psychotherapy and
  Counselling at Regent's College   Tel: 0207 487 7446; spc@regents.ac.uk
The Stoic Foundation   cyberstoic@aol.com
Tim LeBon   timlebon@aol.com

Index